HIKING THE TOUR OF MONTE ROSA

TREKKING THE SWISS AND ITALIAN ALPS FROM ZERMATT

By Maddy Williams

JUNIPER HOUSE, MURLEY MOSS,
OXENHOLME ROAD, KENDAL, CUMBRIA LA9 7RL
www.cicerone.co.uk

First edition 2025
ISBN: 978 1 78631 266 2
eISBN: 978 1 78765 204 0

Printed in Singapore by KHL Printing on responsibly sourced paper.
A catalogue record for this book is available from the British Library.
All photographs are by the author or Jonathan Williams unless otherwise stated.

Route mapping by Lovell Johns www.lovelljohns.com
Contains OpenStreetMap.org data © OpenStreetMap contributors, CC-BY-SA. NASA relief data courtesy of ESRI

Cicerone's representative for GPSR compliance is Easy Access System Europe, Mustamäe tee 50, 10621 Tallinn, Estonia. Email gpsr.requests@easproject.com.

Updates to this guide

While every effort is made by our authors to ensure the accuracy of guidebooks as they go to print, changes can occur during the lifetime of an edition. Any updates that we know of for this guide will be on the Cicerone website (www.cicerone.co.uk/1266/updates), so please check before planning your trip. We also advise that you check information about such things as transport, accommodation and shops locally. Even rights of way can be altered over time.

The route maps in this guide are derived from publicly available data, databases and crowd-sourced data. As such they have not been through the detailed checking procedures that would generally be applied to a published map from an official mapping agency, although naturally we have reviewed them closely in the light of local knowledge as part of the preparation of this guide.

We are always grateful for information about any discrepancies between a guidebook and the facts on the ground, sent by email to updates@cicerone.co.uk.

Register your book: To sign up to receive free updates, special offers and GPX files where available, create a Cicerone account and register your purchase via the 'My Account' tab at www.cicerone.co.uk.

Front cover: A hiker on the Europaweg above the Mattertal, with views of the monumental Weisshorn (Stage 10)

CONTENTS

Mountain safety . . . 5
Map key . . . 6
Route summary table . . . 7
Overview profile and sample itineraries . . . 8
Stage facilities planner . . . 10

INTRODUCTION . . . 15
The Tour of Monte Rosa – overview . . . 16
Route and schedule options . . . 20

Planning your trip . . . 24
Experience and preparation . . . 24
What to take . . . 25
When to go . . . 26
Where to stay . . . 27
Using this guide . . . 30

Essential information . . . 32
Sustainable travel . . . 32
Getting there and back . . . 32
Weather . . . 37
Food . . . 38
Money . . . 39
Languages . . . 39
Waymarks and route finding . . . 39
Maps and apps . . . 40
Safety in the mountains . . . 42
Glacier crossing . . . 44

The Monte Rosa region . . . 47
History and culture . . . 47
The Walser . . . 49
Monte Rosa and the Golden Age of Mountaineering . . . 51
Geology . . . 53
Wildlife and flowers . . . 53

THE TOUR OF MONTE ROSA . . . 57
Stage 1 Zermatt to Gandegghütte . . . 58
Stage 2 Gandegghütte to Resy . . . 65
Stage 3 Resy to Alpe Gabiet . . . 73

Stage 4 Alpe Gabiet to Rifugio Pastore . . . 80
Stage 5 Rifugio Pastore to Macugnaga . . . 87
Stage 6 Macugnaga to Monte Moro (Rifugio Oberto Maroli) . . . 93
Stage 7A Monte Moro to Saas-Fee . . . 98
Stage 7 Monte Moro to Britanniahütte . . . 105
Stage 8 Britanniahütte to Saas-Fee . . . 112
Stage 9 Saas-Fee to Grächen . . . 117
Stage 10 Grächen to Europahütte . . . 123
Stage 11 Europahütte to Zermatt . . . 130

Appendix A Accommodation . . . 138
Appendix B Useful contacts . . . 144
Appendix C Further reading . . . 146
Appendix D Italian–German–English glossary . . . 148

For all the Cicerone authors; past, present and future.

Acknowledgements

Thanks first and foremost must go to Jonathan Williams, who came along on research trips for this guide, offered authorly advice and took a look over drafts. Thanks also to the other Williamses; Joe for commissioning this new guide for Monte Rosa, and Lesley for more author insights.

Hiking the Tour of Monte Rosa isn't a new guide for Cicerone, and I follow in the footsteps of other authors before me; thanks are due to Hilary Sharp's excellent and informative previous editions, and Chris Wright's epic *Grand Tour of Monte Rosa* – a far greater undertaking than this!

Writing this guide has not only been about love of the TMR and wanting to share this incredible trek with others, but it has also been about stepping into the shoes of a Cicerone author; a new – and hopefully valuable – perspective for a publisher. Thank you to those who have taken these pieces and crafted them into a book; my editor Nicole Spray, copy-editor Helen Johnson, and designer Clare Crooke. And to the rest of the Cicerone team for all their support.

Mountain safety

Every mountain walk has its dangers, and those described in this guidebook are no exception. All who walk or climb in the mountains should recognise this and take responsibility for themselves and their companions along the way. The author and publisher have made every effort to ensure that the information contained in this guide was correct when it went to press, but, except for any liability that cannot be excluded by law, they cannot accept responsibility for any loss, injury or inconvenience sustained by any person using this book.

International distress signal *(emergency only)*
Six blasts on a whistle (and flashes with a torch after dark) spaced evenly for one minute, followed by a minute's pause. Repeat until an answer is received. The response is three signals per minute followed by a minute's pause.

Helicopter rescue
The following signals are used to communicate with a helicopter:

Help needed: raise both arms above head to form a 'Y'

Help not needed: raise one arm above head, extend other arm downward

Emergency telephone numbers
If telephoning from abroad the dialling codes are:
Italy: 0039; *Switzerland:* 0041
Emergency Services:
Italy: tel 118 or 112; *Switzerland:* OCVS (Organisation Cantonale Valaisanne de Secours): tel 144 or 112

Weather reports
General: www.mountain-forecast.com
Switzerland: tel 162 (in French, German or Italian), www.meteoschweiz.ch/en

Mountain rescue can be very expensive – be adequately insured.

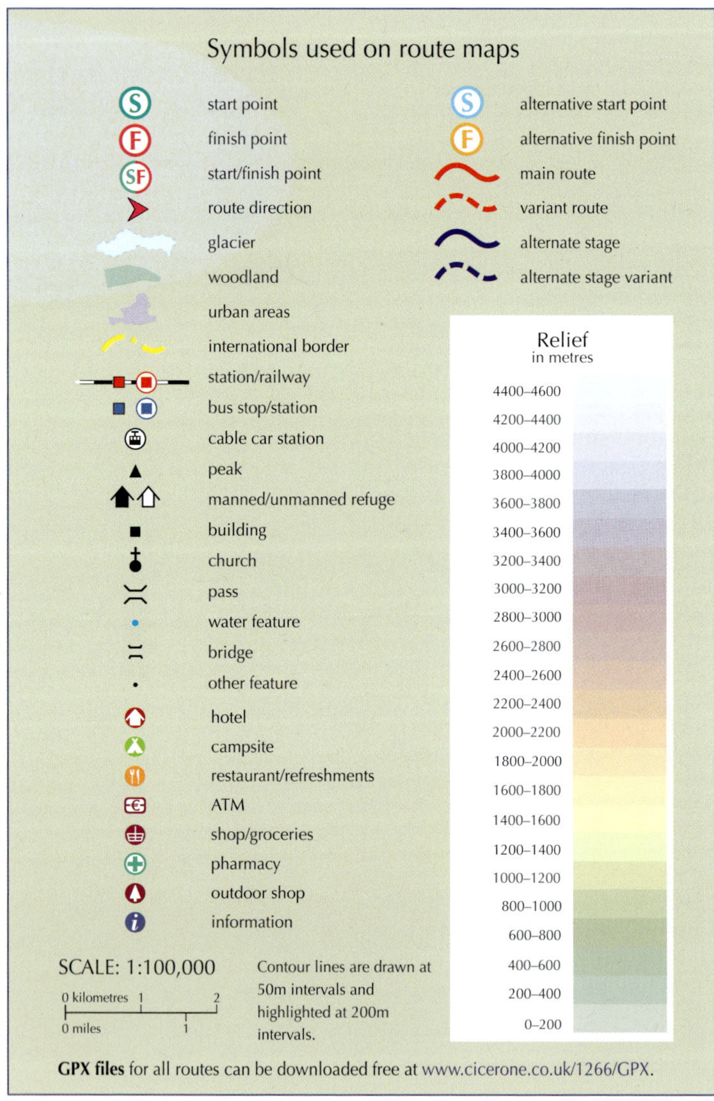
Symbols used on route maps
start point
finish point
start/finish point
route direction
glacier
woodland
urban areas
international border
station/railway
bus stop/station
cable car station
peak
manned/unmanned refuge
building
church
pass
water feature
bridge
other feature
hotel
campsite
restaurant/refreshments
ATM
shop/groceries
pharmacy
outdoor shop
information
alternative start point
alternative finish point
main route
variant route
alternate stage
alternate stage variant
Relief
in metres
4400–4600
4200–4400
4000–4200
3800–4000
3600–3800
3400–3600
3200–3400
3000–3200
2800–3000
2600–2800
2400–2600
2200–2400
2000–2200
1800–2000
1600–1800
1400–1600
1200–1400
1000–1200
800–1000
600–800
400–600
200–400
0–200
SCALE: 1:100,000
0 kilometres 1 2
0 miles 1
Contour lines are drawn at 50m intervals and highlighted at 200m intervals.
GPX files for all routes can be downloaded free at www.cicerone.co.uk/1266/GPX.

ROUTE SUMMARY TABLE

Stage	Start	Finish	Time (hr min)	Distance (km)	Ascent (m)	Descent (m)	Page no.
1	Zermatt	Gandegghütte	4hr 10min	10.5	1450	35	58
2	Gandegghütte	Resy	7hr	20.5	680	1640	65
3	Resy	Alpe Gabiet	5hr 30min	14.7	1285	1000	73
4	Alpe Gabiet	Rif Pastore	7hr	18.3	990	1765	80
5	Rif Pastore	Macugnaga	7hr 30min	22.0	1245	1505	87
6	Macugnaga	Monte Moro	4hr	7.6	1490	10	93
7A	Monte Moro	Saas-Fee	5hr 20min	17.2	300	1295	98
7	Monte Moro	Britanniahütte	6hr	14.0	1040	810	105
8	Britanniahütte	Saas-Fee	3hr 40min	10.2	100	1325	112
9	Saas-Fee	Grächen	7hr 10min	20.3	995	1180	117
10	Grächen	Europahütte	6hr 35min	17.0	1455	805	123
11	Europahütte	Zermatt	6hr 25min	19.5	765	1420	130
Total (via Britanniahütte)			65hr	174.6	11,495	11,495	
Total (direct to Saas-Fee – 7A)			60hr 40min	167.6	10,655	10,655	

OVERVIEW PROFILE AND SAMPLE ITINERARIES

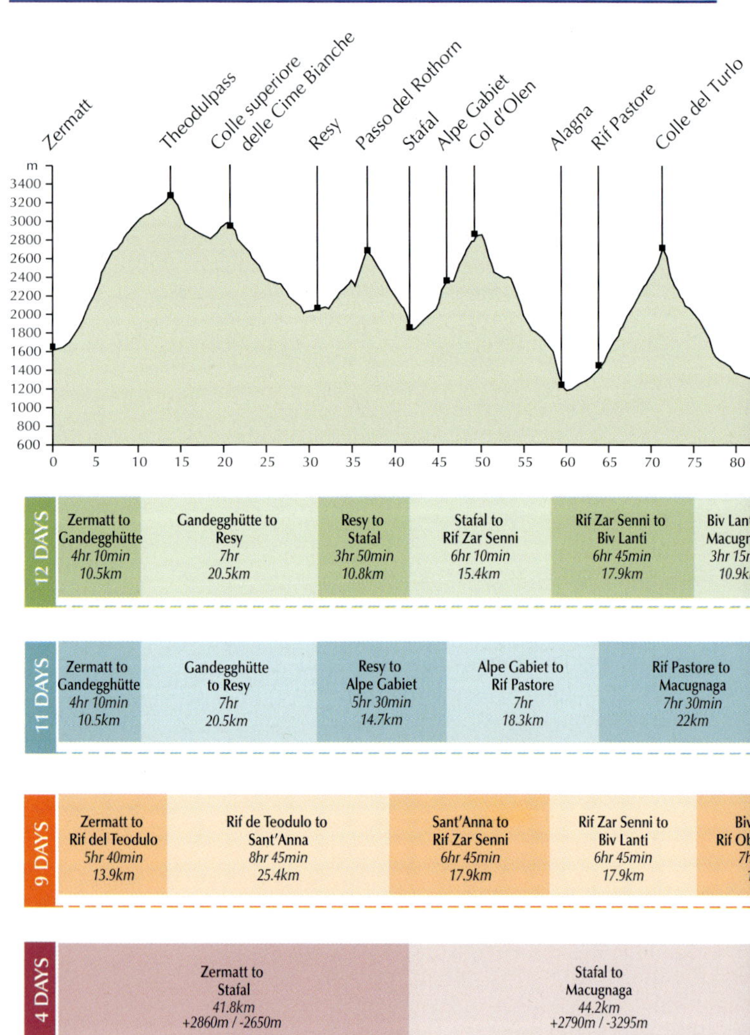

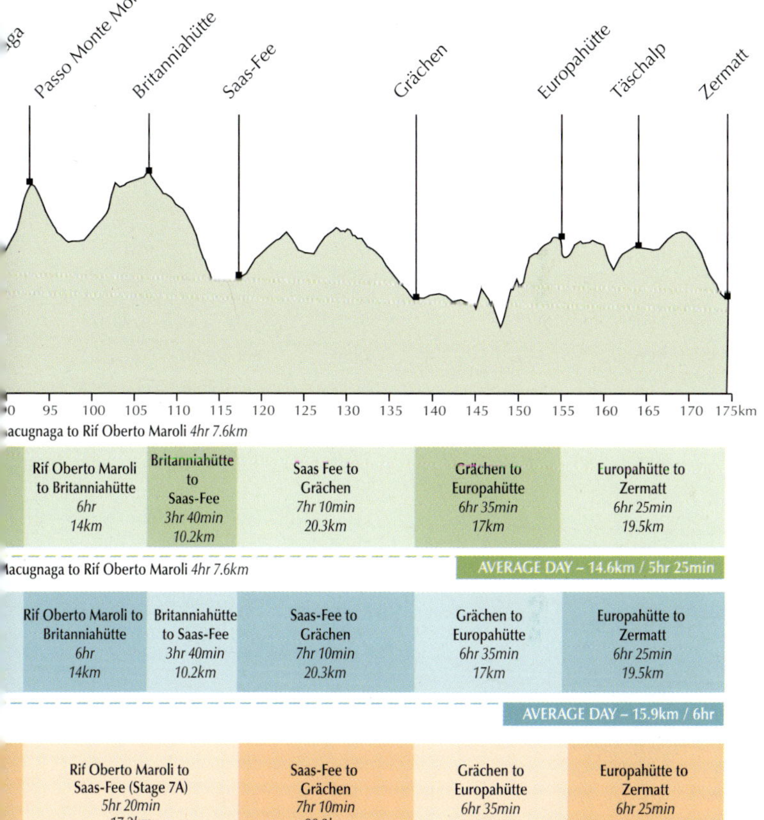

Macugnaga to Grächen (Stage 7A)
45.1km
+2785m / -2485m

Grächen to Zermatt
36.5km
+2220m / -2225m

FASTPACKING ITINERARY AVERAGE DAY – 41.9km

STAGE FACILITIES PLANNER

Stage	Place	Altitude (m)	Walking time
1	**Zermatt**	**1616**	**-**
1	Furi	1862	0hr 55min
1	Trockener Steg	2929	2hr 50min
1	**Gandegghütte**	**3028**	**25min**
2	Rif del Teodulo	3319	1hr 30min
2	Laghi delle Cime Bianche	2808	1hr 10min
2	*Saint-Jacques*	*1689*	*+40min from main route, 3hr 50min from Cime Bianche, +1hr onwards to Resy*
2	**Resy**	**2066**	**4hr 20min**
3	Sant'Anna	2190	3hr 15min
3	Stafal	1818	35min
3	**Alpe Gabiet**	**2350**	**1hr 40min**
3	*Rif Gabiet*	*2357*	*+10min and +0.3km from Alpe Gabiet*
3	*Oresteshütte*	*2600*	*+50min and +3km from Alpe Gabiet. +30min to rejoin the TMR on Stage 4*
4	Rif Zar Senni	1664	4hr 30min
4	Alagna	1191	1hr
4	**Rif Pastore**	**1575**	**1hr 30min**
5	Biv Lanti	2125	4hr 15min
5	Quarazza	1324	2hr 30min
5	**Macugnaga**	**1315**	**45min**
6	Rif Scarteboden	1515	30min
6	Alpe Bill	1700	35min
6	**Rif Oberto Maroli**	**2796**	**2hr 55min**
7	**Britanniahütte**	**3027**	**6hr**
8	Plattjen	2570	2hr

refuge/hut · unmanned hut · hotel · camping · restaurant/refreshments · ATM · shop/groceries · pharmacy · outdoor shop · TIC · train · bus · lift/cable car

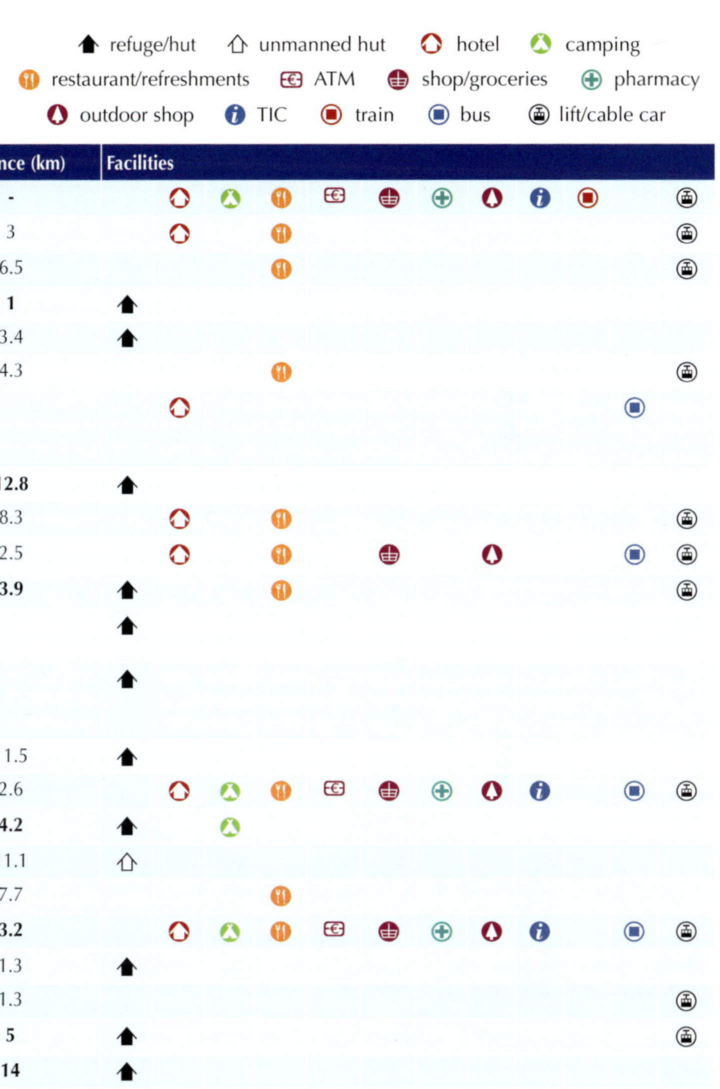

istance (km)	Facilities											
-		hotel	camping	restaurant/refreshments	ATM	shop/groceries	pharmacy	outdoor shop	TIC	train		lift/cable car
3		hotel		restaurant/refreshments								lift/cable car
6.5				restaurant/refreshments								lift/cable car
1	refuge/hut											
3.4	refuge/hut											
4.3				restaurant/refreshments								lift/cable car
		hotel									bus	
12.8	refuge/hut											
8.3		hotel		restaurant/refreshments								lift/cable car
2.5		hotel		restaurant/refreshments		shop/groceries		outdoor shop			bus	lift/cable car
3.9	refuge/hut			restaurant/refreshments								lift/cable car
	refuge/hut											
	refuge/hut											
11.5	refuge/hut											
2.6		hotel	camping	restaurant/refreshments	ATM	shop/groceries	pharmacy	outdoor shop	TIC		bus	lift/cable car
4.2	refuge/hut		camping									
11.1	unmanned hut											
7.7				restaurant/refreshments								
3.2		hotel	camping	restaurant/refreshments	ATM	shop/groceries	pharmacy	outdoor shop	TIC		bus	lift/cable car
1.3	refuge/hut											
1.3												lift/cable car
5	refuge/hut											lift/cable car
14	refuge/hut											
4.7				restaurant/refreshments								lift/cable car

Stage	Place	Altitude (m)	Walking time
8	**Saas-Fee**	**1803**	**1hr 40min**
9	Hannigalp	2122	6hr 15min
9	Z'Seew	1721	45min
9	**Grächen**	**1618**	**10min**
10	Gasenried	1660	35min
10	*Herbriggen*	*1261*	*+10min from main route, 2hr 45min from Gasenried*
10	**Europahütte**	**2264**	**6hr**
11	Täschalp	2175	3hr 25min
11	Tufteren	2215	1hr 45min
11	**Zermatt**	**1616**	**1hr 15min**
7A	Rif Oberto Maroli	2796	–
7A	Mattmark	2204	2hr 45min
7A	Saas-Almagell	1671	1hr 45min
7A	**Saas-Fee**	**1803**	**50min**

The Rimpfischhorn and Strahlhorn rise above a morning cloud inversion viewed from Gandegghütte (Stage 1/2)

istance (km)	Facilities
5.5	
17.2	
2.4	
0.7	
2.4	
14.6	
9.2	
6.2	
4.1	
–	
7.7	
6.2	
3.3	

The Matterhorn's east face and Hörnli ridge towers above the path at Furggbach (Stage 1)

INTRODUCTION

Dawn light on Monte Rosa (Piramide Vincent (left), Parrotspitze (centre), and Signalkuppe (right, highest)) from Rif Pastore (Stages 4/5)

The silence is broken by a gasp – 'look!'

There, silhouetted against the rising sun, a young ibex picks her way delicately along a shelf of rock. The Mattertal far below is filled with a thick cushion of cloud, only the highest peaks breaking free. It is cold, and we have only just left the cosy glow of the hut to climb up the Theodul, but the towers and spires of the mountains are warming from grey to gold in the dawn and the sight of the ibex is an unexpected gift in this Alpine amphitheatre. A perfect start to the day.

This is the Tour of Monte Rosa (TMR); moments of splendour, joy, adventure and warm camaraderie strung along a ribbon around the massif. Nowhere else in the Alps can you find more 4000m summits, and the TMR ventures higher than other alpine trekking routes, crossing glaciers and high passes over 3000m. Is it a challenge? Of course. There are long days, steep and wearying climbs, tricky terrain to clamber through and dizzying drops beside the paths. But those who take on this challenge will be rewarded by some of the best mountain trekking to be found, and the cheery hospitality of mountain huts and villages in Switzerland and Italy.

The cross-border circuit of the Monte Rosa follows in centuries-old footsteps between valleys and over the Swiss–Italian border via the Theodul and Monte Moro passes. The landscape itself has defined the culture and history of this region, which persists to this day in the care and preservation of the land. Monte Rosa dominates the skyline throughout the trek – each day a different vantage point, with different summits of the massif and Mischabel range in view. The Matterhorn, Breithorn, Liskamm, Dom, Rimpfischhorn, Weisshorn – this is a hike among the giants of the Alps; seven of the top ten highest Alpine peaks accompany the journey.

Nor are the lower slopes any less spectacular; pastures are strewn with colourful flowers, and the toll of cow bells can be heard as the route traces the path of perfectly clear streams. Sunlight filters through forests that smell rich with resin and pine, and welcoming villages of ancient timber and stone buildings cluster beneath the snowy horizon.

For those who walk the Tour of Monte Rosa, this guide aims to inform and inspire you for the route. But it is the unexpected – friendships made with other hikers, a chance spotting of an ibex, even a day spent waiting-out the weather – which can give the greatest rewards.

THE TOUR OF MONTE ROSA – OVERVIEW

As a 175km loop, the TMR can start at any point, but for the purposes of this guidebook it begins in the famed Swiss-Valais mountain town

Monte Rosa and the Gornergletscher, with Liskamm on the right, on the walk towards Trockener Steg (Stage 1)

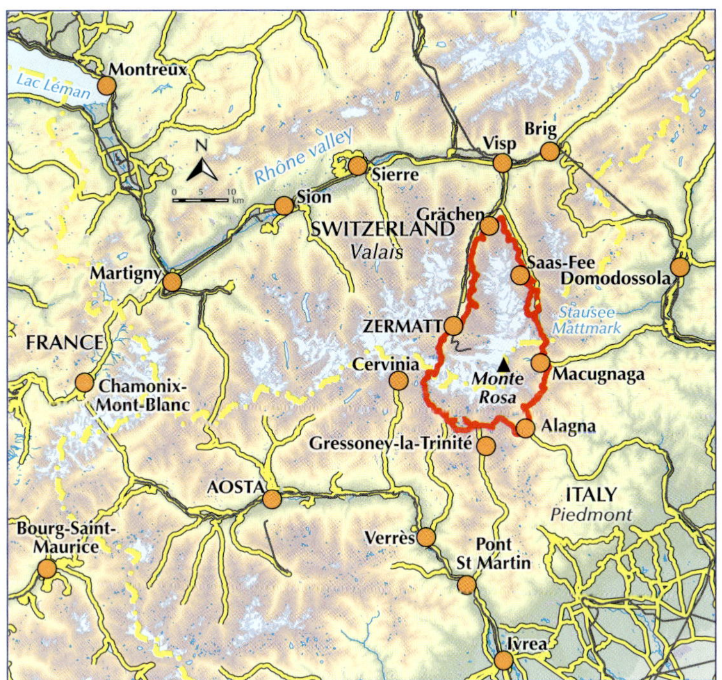

of Zermatt, in the shadow of the Matterhorn. Zermatt lies in a mountain amphitheatre among a collection of the highest and most spectacular mountains in the Alps, and the first day of climbing south towards Gandegghütte and Rifugio del Teodulo, on the border with Italy, is surrounded by views of more 4000m peaks than at any other time on the trail.

The crossing into Italy is over the Theodulpass (3295m), a historic route connecting Italy with the Valais, with the TMR leading over the Theodulgletscher. This glacier is used as a ski piste throughout the year, and the trail is simple to follow, but can be skipped by cable car if conditions are poor or if hikers would prefer to avoid the glacier crossing. Despite the splendour of the southern and eastern faces of the Matterhorn, the first few kilometres in Italy are unfortunately some of the least attractive parts of the TMR, as works on the ski area above Cervinia have left their mark. The next pass, the Colle Superiore delle

Ibex grazing under rosy light at dusk from the Britanniahütte, with the Strahlhorn (left) and Rimpfischhorn (centre-right) (Stages 7/8)

Cime Bianche (2982m) brings the trail into the upper reaches of the Val d'Ayas and views up to the Breithorn, Castor and Pollux, and a long descent through green, flower-strewn meadows, past turquoise lakes and clear streams to the two rifugios in the hamlet of Resy.

Stage 3 of the TMR has a choice of pass: the Passo del Rothorn (2689m), and the Colle di Bettaforca (2675m). The Rothorn, a wild and picturesque climb, is the preferable route unless hikers wish to take a chairlift some – or all – of the way. The trail now enters the Gressoney, or Lys Valley, overlooked by the snow-bound bulk of Liskamm, before climbing the eastern flank of the valley to the dispersed buildings and mountain huts of Alpe Gabiet and the dammed Lago Gabiet.

The route into Valsesia and the town of Alagna first climbs the Col d'Olen (2881m), before dropping through pastures frequented by ibex towards Passo Foric (2432m), which passes over a long and spectacular ridgeline. The descent to Alagna drops through several Walser hamlets; beautiful examples of traditional architecture. Alagna is one of the few towns visited in Italy and is worth exploring.

From Alagna, the trail follows the Fiume Sesia river north to Rifugio Pastore, and the grand sight of Monte Rosa's Signalkuppe, Parrotspitze and Piramide Vincent summits, and then begins one of the great passes on the trail, over the Colle del Turlo (2738m). The Turlo has been in use for centuries – as with other cols on the Italian side, notably for migration and inter-valley connection by the Walser communities – and in the 1930s it was further improved by the construction of a rock and slab track along the entire route to Macugnaga.

Macugnaga in the Valle Anzasca sits at the foot of the immense east face of Monte Rosa, the largest mountain wall in the Alps. The himalayan view of the face accompanies the long grind of the climb north to the Rifugio Oberto Maroli and Passo Monte Moro at 2872m. Like its counterpart at the Theodulpass, the Monte Moro is another historic route connecting Italy with the Valais and is topped with a golden statue – the Madonna of the Snows – which gazes back to Monte Rosa.

From the Monte Moro, hikers have a choice: a two-day route via the 3027m Britanniahütte and crossing the Allalingletscher and Hohlaubgletscher to Saas-Fee, a route which rewards trekkers with immense views over glaciers and rock to the 4000m Allalinhorn, Strahlhorn and Rimpfischhorn; or alternatively, a lower-level, one-day route through to the mountain resort. Saas-Fee sits above the Saastal in a cirque of the Mischabel peaks, including the highest mountain entirely in Switzerland – the Dom (as the highest summit of Monte Rosa is shared with Italy).

From Saas-Fee, the final three days of the TMR follow the Swiss Tour of Monte Rosa, or Swiss Route 27. These three days comprise some of the best balcony routes to be found, as the trail first follows the Grächen Höhenweg as it clings to the sheer slopes of the Saastal, 1000m above the valley floor. The route reaches the northern-most point of the TMR, where the Mattertal and Saastal valleys meet, before turning southwards again to the small town of Grächen.

The finale of the trail back to Zermatt follows the challenging Europaweg, as it winds above the Mattertal with bridges, ropes, cables, tunnels and a crossing of the Charles Kuonen suspension bridge: half a kilometre long, the longest suspension bridge in the Alps. The two days of the Europaweg can be broken with a stay at the Europahütte and are accompanied by outstanding views as the Mattertal peaks appear, one by one, before the final descent into Zermatt and the completion of the Tour of Monte Rosa.

THE CROWN OF MONTE ROSA

The Queen of the Alps, Monte Rosa is the second highest mountain in the range, as well as the largest massif with the highest concentration of 4000m peaks in Europe. Unlike Mont Blanc, Monte Rosa is not just one summit but claims 22 separate 4000m peaks in the entire group (the main summit cluster, as well as the ridge of peaks which stretches from the Theodulpass to Passo Monte Moro), making an enormous and elaborate crown to the massif.

The highest peak is Dufourspitze, at 4634m, closely followed by its nearest neighbours, Dunantspitze (4632m), Grenzgipfel (4618m), Nordend

(4609m) and Zumsteinspitze (4563m). Following the ridge to the south are Signalkuppe/Punta Gnifetti (4554m), Parrotspitze/Punta Parrot (4434m), Ludwigshöhe (4343m) with nearby Piramide Vincent/Vincentpiramid) (4215m) and Corno Nero/Schwarzhorn (4322m) wholly in Italy.

Further along the border ridge is the icy bulk of Liskamm (4532m), Castor (4225m) Pollux (4089m) and the Breithorn (4160m). Different peaks will dominate the views day by day on the TMR, with the very best views of Monte Rosa on Stages 1/2 on the ascent from Zermatt, and Stages 6/7 with views of the monumental east face.

ROUTE AND SCHEDULE OPTIONS

There are several choices when planning your TMR; which way round to go, where to start, and whether to avoid the glaciers. Options are outlined below.

The information on facilities and route options in this guide are provided to give the hiker the greatest scope to define their own TMR itinerary; whether that involves using cable cars, planning shorter stages to allow time to explore the local area, or longer stages for fastpackers. However, there are some stages which cannot reasonably be shortened. These include Stage 5, over the Turlo, which is a long day of 22km between Valsesia and Valle Anzasca, and Stages 9, 10, and 11 along the Grächen Höhenweg and Europaweg. Anyone planning to hike the TMR should therefore be prepared for consecutive, long days of alpine walking.

Anti-clockwise or clockwise

As a circuit, the TMR can be walked in either direction. The description in this guide is written anti-clockwise, which, after consideration, is the preferable way to go. For one, it is hard to see how to improve upon the final three days of the TMR covering the traversing routes from Saas-Fee to Zermatt on the Grächen Höhenweg and the Europaweg. As this is some of the most technical terrain on the trek, it is better to finish rather than start with it.

Going anti-clockwise also avoids particularly arduous clockwise days such as 15km of 1500m from Macugnaga to the Colle del Turlo, followed the next day by 15km and 1700m ascent from Rif Pastore to Col d'Olen. This means that going anti-clockwise, those routes are taken as descents, but the benefit in walking time is worth understanding: a clockwise Macugnaga to Rif Pastore over the Turlo could take over 8hr 30min (which does not include time for breaks) instead of 7hr 30min, and Pastore to Gabiet over Col d'Olen could take 8hr instead of the anti-clockwise 7hr.

If you do opt for the clockwise route, aim to stay at Rif del Teodulo rather than Gandegghütte; as it will be better to cross the glacier in the morning when the ice is most stable.

Start and finish options

There is no gentle start to the TMR, but some start points are easier to get to than others. Zermatt has the best transport options into the Swiss rail system, and the first day climbing south towards the Theodulpass is not overly long or technical and rewards your effort with a succession of immense views. Zermatt is also the largest town en route and offers plenty to do and explore before and after the trail. Starting here also means that you can enjoy the three extraordinary days from Saas-Fee traversing above the valley as a fitting finish to the Tour.

A start in Italy is also possible, with each valley served by regular local buses (see 'Getting there and back'). Either the Valle d'Ayas (St Jacques/Resy), Valle del Lys (Gressoney/Stafal) or Valle Anzasca (Macugnaga) are potential start options. Alagna and Valsesia would be more challenging, requiring a long, 22km day over the Colle del Turlo on the first day.

No-glacier option

Before summer 2023, there was no way around the glacier crossing of the Theodulgletscher. With the opening of the cable car from Switzerland to Italy, the TMR has become far more

Looking back at the Passo del Rothorn and Bloabhòre (left) reflected in the Laghetti del Salero (Stage 3)

Well placed benches offer unparalleled lunchtime views (Stage 1)

accessible for hikers, as it is now possible to complete the Tour without going over glaciers.

Whether you are unsure about crossing glaciers, don't want to add the weight of spikes to your pack, or if weather and glacier conditions deteriorate, the TMR can be walked without stepping foot onto the ice. For the Theodulgletscher on Stage 2, this means taking the Matterhorn Glacier Ride cable car from Trockener Steg (or all the way from Zermatt) over to Laghi delle Cime Bianche, in Italy. Be warned, this isn't a cheap trip.

For the crossing of the Allalingletscher and Hohlaubgletscher on Stage 7, this can be entirely avoided by walking the alternative, lower-level route between Monte Moro and Saas-Fee (Stage 7A), which saves a day on the trail.

Cable car and gondola options for a week-long trek

If you are short on time, the TMR can be condensed into seven to eight days by using cable car and lift options. This is to illustrate what is possible, rather than a recommendation: the delights of a trek are in the journey after all. An example itinerary would be:

1. *Cable car from Zermatt to Cime Bianche,* walk to Resy
2. *Lifts over the Bettaforca to Stafal, and optionally to Alpe Gabiet,* walk to Rif Zar Senni
3. Walk to Bivacco Lanti (unmanned)
4. Walk to Macugnaga, *cable car to Monte Moro,* walk to Mattmark, *bus to Saas-Almagell,* walk or bus to Saas-Fee
5. Walk to Grächen
6. Walk to Europahütte
7. Walk to Zermatt

THE UTMR

Beginning in 2015, the Tour of Monte Rosa has staged an annual ultra-marathon trail race known as the Ultra Tour Monte Rosa (UTMR) in the first week of September. In a similar fashion to the highly popular Ultra Tour du Mont Blanc (UTMB), the UTMR comprises a number of different trail running races, with the flagship event a non-stop race of the entire TMR route starting in Grächen. There is also a stage race, where runners break the trail into four days; this itinerary is included on the 'Overview profile' for fastpackers. More information about the UTMR is available at www.ultra-tourmonterosa.com.

The current route of the UTMR mirrors the TMR trekking route except for the following diversions:

- Stage 1, the UTMR bypasses Furi and goes through Hermetje, a small detour
- Stage 3, the UTMR leaves the TMR at Sant'Anna and descends Route 9 to Gressoney-la-Trinité and then climbs straight from Gressoney to Alpe Gabiet on Route 4
- Stage 4, a small diversion which bypasses the Col d'Olen and continues up the access track further north to the Passo dei Salati, before rejoining the TMR on the eastern side of the passes
- And from Monte Moro, the UTMR follows Stage 7A along Mattmarksee and into the Saastal

PLANNING YOUR TRIP

The sweeping ridgelines of Passo Foric and the Italian Alps from the Col d'Olen (Stage 4)

EXPERIENCE AND PREPARATION

The TMR is an incredible Alpine trek, but it's one of the more challenging ones. With an average ascent and descent of 1000m per day, with walking time up to 7hr 30min, there are unavoidable back-to-back, long and technical days of walking. As such, the better your fitness and preparation before you go; the more you will enjoy the experience.

While the TMR is a similar distance to the Tour du Mont Blanc, it has over 1000m more ascent and descent. It also spends more time at altitude, crosses higher passes, and travels over a couple of glaciers. It's an excellent choice for those who are looking for what's next after having enjoyed a previous trek like the Tour du Mont Blanc, or the Chamonix–Zermatt route. Or for mountaineers who are looking for a varied, non-technical trek.

The glaciers the TMR crosses are relatively 'user friendly' but shouldn't be underestimated. If you have never travelled on glaciers before, it is highly recommended to hire a guide and/or get training beforehand (see 'Glacier crossing').

You should have a good level of fitness before you go. There is nothing better than walking as preparation; a few consecutive long walks before you go – preferably with a similar sized backpack to what you will trek with – will certainly help.

Once you have travelled to Monte Rosa to start the TMR, it's a very good idea to spend a couple of days walking, acclimatising and sleeping at altitude before you begin the TMR.

What to take

Every hiker will have their own preference, but luckily, with new innovations making outdoor gear lighter all the time, it's possible now to have everything you need for a trek in a 25–35l backpack, weighing 4–6kg (without food and water). Some essentials for the trail include:

- Boots, which fit you properly, with good ankle support and grip (such as Vibram soles). Some hikers may prefer using trail running shoes, but this is only recommended if you're an experienced trail runner.
- Waterproof shell, top and bottom. It's likely that you'll get some rain along the TMR, especially in the Italian valleys. Take the best and lightest waterproofs you have, they will potentially need to withstand a full day of relentless rain. When not raining, they can also give you another layer and act as a windproof.
- Hiking clothes; travelling light is important, but it's best to also have a spare set in case of getting caught in rain or when clothes need a wash. Typical trekking clothes for the TMR are shorts or hiking trousers/leggings, and short- or long-sleeved base layers.
- The mornings and evenings can be chilly at altitude, and weather can be unpredictable. Take a warm fleece or similar layer, as well as a hat and gloves for colder temperatures.
- Sunshine and heat is as important to prepare for as the cold; a brimmed hat, sunglasses and sun cream are essentials. Some trekkers also prefer to cover up with highly breathable layers.
- In most cases, mountain huts provide hut shoes for you to wear, but it's useful to take a light pair of shoes or sandals for when you're staying in a town.
- Sleeping bag liner (silk is the best option) for staying in refuges, these are compulsory in Alpine Club huts.
- A small first-aid kit is essential, and should contain antiseptic wipes and cream, plasters/band-aids, wound dressings, blister plasters (Compeed), insect bite cream, tweezers, and painkillers. An emergency bivi sack is highly recommended in case of accidents to keep you warm and protected. Also useful are a couple of wilderness wipes/wet wipes for when staying in a hut without showers, and travel wash for laundry.

- Remember your travel essentials: money, passport, and insurance information.
- Other useful items to take include chargers for electronic devices (you may need a European type-C adaptor), penknife, head torch, compass, maps and guidebook.
- Water bottles or hydration systems: drinking water is readily available so a water filter isn't a requirement. You ought to aim for around 1.5 to 2l of capacity.
- Trekking poles are incredibly useful for all sorts of different terrain, and can give you a little more stability over uneven ground and glaciers, and more support for long downhills.
- Crampons/Spikes: if you plan to cross one or both glacier options on the TMR, then spikes are essential. Microspikes that fit over your boots will give you enough grip in good conditions, or 10-point crampons for a little extra spike. While these are extra weight, it is far better to take them than find yourself unprepared on a glacier.
- Optional: gaiters, rope, axe, if you plan a little mountaineering along the route or are likely to face a 'wet' glacier; tent/other backpacking gear if you plan to camp.

WHEN TO GO

The summer trekking season in the Alps is bookmarked by the level of remaining winter snow in June, and the onset of the cold autumn weather in September. This is broadly mirrored by the opening and closure times of the mountain huts en route. While there is some variability here, the high huts over 3000m generally open mid to late June, and close early to mid September.

June

Expect a lot of snow on the ground on the passes and at higher altitude, there can be more snow in June than in January. While there have been some years where hot spring and early summer weather have cleared much from the ground, the opposite is just as likely, with mountaineering conditions on the passes and wet (snow-covered) glaciers through into July. If you go in June, bring crampons and potentially rope and an ice-axe, or be prepared for the need to find alternative routes if the paths need technical equipment to be safe. Huts will generally open for the season mid to late June, and the staff can advise on the current walking conditions.

July

All huts and cable cars should be open, with pastures filled with alpine flowers. It's likely that remaining snow on the passes will still be clearing throughout the month. It is also school holiday time in both Italy and Switzerland, so expect popular areas to be busy.

The final section of the Europaweg walks straight towards the Matterhorn (Stage 11)

August

Between mid July and the end of August is some of the best time for summer trekking. All but the most tenacious snow cover should be gone. The Swiss school holidays end mid-month, but this is also a popular time for visiting the Alps, so booking ahead is advised. Afternoon thunderstorms are a little more common in August, and the weather can turn cold with autumn storms at the end of the month.

September

A much quieter TMR can be had in the first half of September, as colder weather moves in and autumn colours spread over the hillsides. Days can still be bright and sunny, but early snow can bring serious complications. Huts will begin to close from early in the month, so you'll need to plan carefully to ensure you're in time for your accommodation.

WHERE TO STAY

The TMR is a classic alpine trek, and you can sleep with a roof over your head for the whole route – cutting down on the weight of a tent, cooking equipment and sleeping bag. Accommodation is split between mountain huts/refuges/rifugios and the wider accommodation options in hostels and hotels in the valley towns.

There are several stages in the TMR where there is only one viable accommodation option (eg the Europahütte on Stage 10), or where there is one preferred option (eg Rif Pastore in Valsesia (Stage 4) or a stay at Britanniahütte (Stage 7)) which can

Britanniahütte (Stage 7)

be popular and potentially booked up. This means that planning your TMR itinerary and booking key huts ahead of time is vital to ensure your trek goes as planned.

Staying in mountain refuges is a quintessential part of Alpine trekking, and there are a few guidelines on etiquette to make the most out of your stay:

- Booking ahead is advised; for peace of mind if nothing else. Either call the hut or send an email (preferably in German or Italian) requesting a reservation. It's a good idea to state that you will be hiking the TMR, and where you will be coming from that day. An estimated arrival time can be useful, as is a warning if you have specific dietary needs.
- Do not wear your boots in the hut or bring in trekking poles or wet gear. Leave these in the boot room or where directed, and use the provided hut shoes (usually crocs) or your own. Those looking after the refuge will thank you for your efforts to keep it spotless.
- Remember to bring you sleeping bag liner / sheet liner. These are now mandatory in most huts for hygiene.
- Let the guardian of the hut know as soon as you've arrived; you will be shown to your room and bed, and they can let you know what time dinner and breakfast will be. Lay out your sleeping bag liner and stake your claim.
- The guardian will usually have your table for dinner and breakfast reserved; a great opportunity to talk about the day with other hikers at your table.
- Pay in the evening if you can; it saves time for everyone in the morning. Most huts will accept cards, but it is advisable to check first and have cash as a back-up.

- If you have not booked a place at the hut for the following night, the refuge staff may be able to call ahead and secure you a bed.
- Many other guests have had long days and may have early starts (particularly if you are staying at the high huts at Gandegg, Teodulo, or Britannia, where other guests may have very early Alpine starts between 2am to 6am). Expect an early night, with lights out and quiet before or by 10pm. Make sure you have everything you need by your bed so you can avoid late-night rustling.
- Thank the team at the hut for a great stay in the morning!

For accommodation options in the valley towns, a few examples are provided in Appendix A. Alternatively you can either contact the local tourist information centre (see Appendix B), or browse the options and book ahead through Booking.com or other similar sites. Prices can range between reasonable and stratospheric; but even considering the high costs in the Swiss towns, a bit of looking can yield a reasonable deal. A few hotels, for instance, also offer beds in small dormitories which are (slightly) more affordable.

A stay at a refuge in Italy is likely to be between €65–75 per person for half-board (dinner, bed and breakfast). In Switzerland, this will be higher, between 80–100 CHF half-board. Some refuges also have private rooms; these will cost more than shared rooms or dormitories.

Aside from the high huts around 3000m, refuges will have shower facilities, although you may need to pay extra for these. In the high huts, water is very scarce and there are no showers or drinking water on tap, so you should expect to pay for bottled water.

Camping

There are limited campsites along the TMR; only in the valley bases, and often requiring a detour away from the route (for example, Saas-Grund has campsites, but Saas-Fee does not). Details on available campsites are listed in Appendix A. Some refuges,

There are many different terms to describe mountain refuges; huts, *Hütte* in German, *rifugio* and *capanna* in Italian. This guide uses several of the terms interchangeably, and all refer to mountain accommodation that can provide refreshment, managed by a staff (usually referred to as the hut's guardian). A *capanna, bivacco* or *Biwak* also can refer to bivouac huts; typically smaller, unmanned with minimal facilities for overnight stays, these are more similar to bothies in the UK, and should be left in the same condition as on arrival if they are visited.

such as the Rif Pastore in Valsesia, may allow hikers to pitch a tent on their grounds, so hikers can also use their facilities and food. If in doubt, contact the hut ahead of time and ask what they will permit. In Switzerland, wild camping is forbidden, except in remote areas above the treeline, and in Italy, wild camping is also prohibited. If you do wild camp, only pitch your tent between sunrise and sunset away from roads and paths. Be sure to take all your waste with you and leave no trace.

USING THIS GUIDE

This guide is designed to give you all the information you need to plan, prepare, and hike the TMR. The Introduction, Stage facilities planner and Overview profile provide key information to help you plan the length of your stages. By outlining all the information about where you can stay along the route, and understanding the time, climbing, and distance involved, you can build your own itinerary, and book your accommodation ahead of time using the information in Appendix A.

Each stage has essential data about the distance, walking time, level of ascent and descent, high point and variant options. Stage information also outlines the main facilities en route, including refreshment stops, grocery shops, and accommodation, combined with an elevation profile and a 1:100,000 map of the route.

The description of each stage is split into sections which correspond to key points along the trail (such as reaching a pass, or a refreshment or accommodation spot), with intermediate data on that section's distance, walking time, ascent and descent. This aims to help hikers define and walk their own itinerary and plan the day ahead.

The **statistics** in this guide have been recorded by using GPS data while walking the trail. The raw data have then been tested for accuracy using map information and signpost times; the result should be a consistent reflection of the elevation, distance, and timing involved.

The **stage timing** provided is walking time only and does not include time for breaks and lunch stops.

The engineered path on the Turlo manoeuvres past boulders and over scree (Stage 5)

The vast east face of Monte Rosa from Rif Oberto Maroli, the largest mountain wall in the Alps (Stages 6/7)

Adding time for breaks can increase the full time on the trail by 25–40% of the day's total, making a day with 7hr of walking time closer to 9hr from start to finish. The timing given is based on experience of walking the trail and consideration of signpost times, but every hiker is likely to have a different pace, so you may find that the indicated times in this guide are either slower than your natural pace, or faster. You will soon get a sense of whether you are a speedier walker or not, and adjust the indicated timings in this guide accordingly.

Any reference to 'left' or 'right' in the route description refers to the direction of travel on an anti-clockwise circuit of the TMR. If 'left' or 'right' is used when describing glaciers or rivers, this relates to the direction of flow. In case of ambiguity, a compass direction is also provided.

The information in this guide is as accurate as it can be at the time of going to print. Inevitably however, facts on the ground can change, particularly on the more vulnerable sections of the TMR where the effects of rockfalls, glaciers and rivers can lead to path diversions or even permanent closures. Essential updates to this guide are available on Cicerone's website, www.cicerone.co.uk, and any information on changes or out-of-date information on the trail or facilities are very gratefully received.

GPX tracks

GPX tracks for the TMR trail described in this guidebook are available to download free at www.cicerone.co.uk/1266/GPX. A GPS device is an excellent aid to navigation but you should also carry a map and compass and know how to use them. GPX files are provided in good faith, but neither the author nor the publisher accepts responsibility for their accuracy.

ESSENTIAL INFORMATION

SUSTAINABLE TRAVEL

The Alps are among the forefront of regions most affected by climate change. The shrinking of the alpine glaciers is happening at an alarming rate, and the views around the mountains are changing every year. It is hard to miss such obvious effects of a warming climate, so it can be useful to consider how visitors can travel and appreciate the landscape sustainably.

The region around Monte Rosa has gone through periods of warming and cooling over the centuries. Currently, the changing climate affects the mountain infrastructure along the TMR; from high huts like the Britanniahütte which has to manage with very restricted water supplies, to high levels of glacier melt and floods that can cause widespread damage on paths, roads and rail. But the region is also one that takes sustainability very seriously: Zermatt has never permitted vehicles with internal combustion engines (from the 1930s onwards, a series of referenda enforced and continued this ban), with Saas-Fee adopting a similar ban in the 1950s, so the Swiss valleys are remarkably free of smog. The valleys on both the Italian and Swiss sides of the border are also ideal for generating hydro-electric power, with many cable cars (like the latest Matterhorn Glacier Ride) operating only on renewable energy, and mountain huts using solar power and other renewables to cut their carbon footprint.

Hiking is among the least impactful activities, but it too can affect the landscape through over-crowding and path erosion. Remember to stay on defined paths where you can, and take any rubbish and waste away with you to leave no trace. It is also worth remembering the sustainable benefits of hiking: going on a trek can bring vital income to remote villages and huts, so there are sustainable livelihoods providing services in the mountains, and funding for local investment (for example through tourist taxes).

The largest impact on the climate from hikers will undoubtedly be emissions generated through travel to the Monte Rosa region. The section below outlines various options to get to the TMR, but if you want to understand more about the impact of different forms of travel, https://ecopassenger.hafas.de is a good comparison site.

GETTING THERE AND BACK

Switzerland

By train

Because of Zermatt's car restrictions, all visitors starting the TMR in Zermatt must arrive by train. The

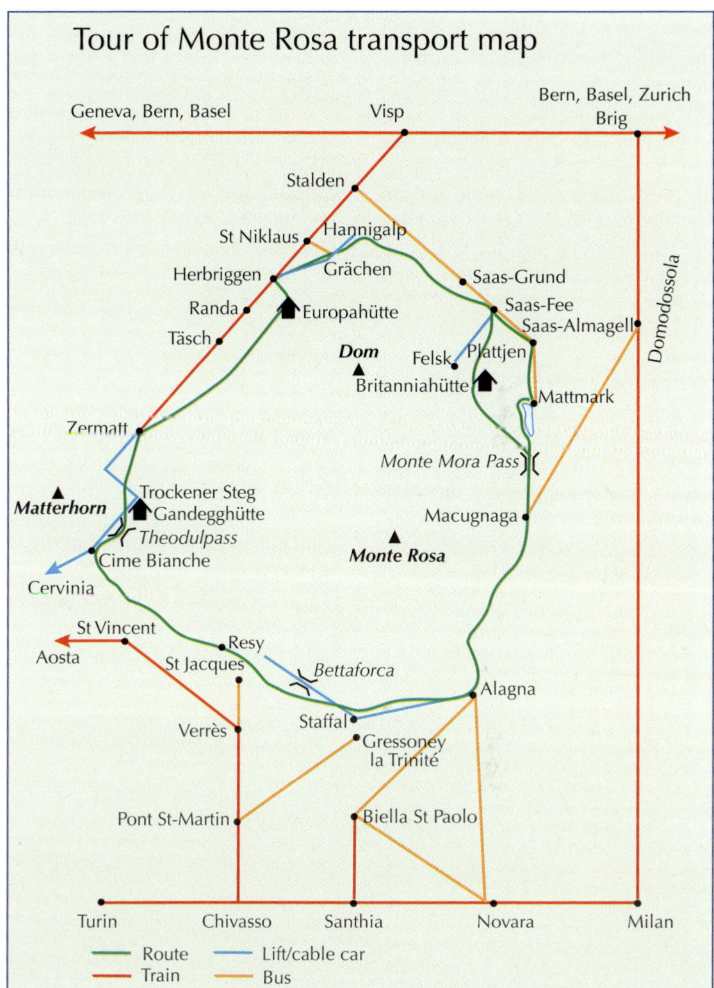

Zermatt railway connects into the wider Swiss rail system at Visp in the Rhône valley. From here, there are direct connections to Geneva, Bern, Basel, and Zurich, providing onward connections to Paris,

Berlin and Munich respectively and the wider European and Eurostar networks. Trains from Visp also connect to Brig, and thence into Italy to Domodossola and the Italian rail system. Trains in Switzerland are some of the most reliable in the world and are operated by SBB. All tickets for trains can be bought through the SBB website www.sbb.ch/en and app, or in stations.

By air

The closest airports to Zermatt are Geneva Airport, Basel (EuroAirport Basel-Mulhouse-Freiburg), and Zurich. Geneva and Zurich have rail access directly from the airport into the Swiss rail system connecting to Zermatt. Basel Airport has regular shuttle buses to Basel Bahnhof (train station).

By bus

Valley buses are usually operated by the PostBus network. They provide valuable connections through into most valleys, towns and villages and align with the rail system.

The closest bus stop to Zermatt is at Täsch (down-valley from Zermatt): all onward travel to Zermatt is by train. Other key bus connections into the Swiss side of the TMR are to Grächen, Saas-Fee, Saas-Almagell, and Mattmark. As with Swiss trains, bus tickets can be booked at www.SBB.ch/en, on the SBB app, or from stations and bus drivers.

By car

To drive on Swiss motorways, you will need a vignette sticker, which has a flat fee (40CHF in 2025) for a year's validity. There are no shorter periods available. As well as the traditional sticker version, you can also buy a digital version (linked to your number plate). Vignettes can be bought at the border, at most petrol stations, and online at www.via.admin.ch/shop.

Saas-Fee and Saas-Grund on the descent from Plattjen (Stage 8)

From France, access to the Swiss Valais is simplest via Geneva and Lausanne, before following the Rhône Valley to Visp, then heading south up the Mattertal. From northern Europe the main highways route through Lucerne on Autobahn 2, and then via the Furkapass (Hauptstrasse 19) or Grimselpass (Hauptstrasse 6) to Visp. As Zermatt is car-free, there is an enormous secure parking facility at Täsch, and at Saas-Fee, which allows for long stays.

Italy

By train

In Italy, trains connect from Turin and Milan (often by a few changes) to: Domodossola for access to Macugnaga and into Switzerland; Biella S. Paolo for access to Alagna; Pont-Saint-Martin for access to the Gressoney valley; and Verrès for the Valle d'Ayas. The onward journey into the valleys is by bus (see below). Trains are operated by TrenItalia and can be booked through their website and app www.trenitalia.com, or via www.thetrainline.com.

By air

In Italy, the most convenient airport hub is Milan, with its three airports: Malpensa, Linate and Bergamo. Malpensa is Milan's main airport, and has both train and bus connections with the city and into the wider Italian train network. A more direct – and often faster – option to get to the mountains is by booking a mini-bus service: Arriva has an 'Airport Line' that connects Milan Malpensa with Verrès and Pont-Saint-Martin in the Valle d'Aosta. Tickets must be pre-booked at https://aosta.arriva.it/en. Alternatively, a shuttle bus operated by Comazzi (Alibus) offers a direct transfer from Malpensa airport to Domodossola, for access to Macugnaga and Switzerland. Pre-booking is required at www.comazzialibus.com.

Linate Airport is close to the centre of Milan, with access to the city via the M4 subway/underground line. Bear in mind that Milan Bergamo is 50km away from the city; there are regular buses to Bergamo station and Milan, as well as connections to other destinations, including the Valle d'Aosta.

By bus

Bus options in Italy are far more numerous than Switzerland, and are the only options for access to, from, and around the Italian valleys. For access to the Valle d'Ayas (Stage 2/3) and Valle del Lys (Stage 3), buses are operated by V.I.T.A. and connect Verrès in the Valle d'Aosta with Champouloc and Saint-Jacques in the Valle d'Ayas, and Pont-Saint-Martin to Stafal/Gressoney. Tickets are available on the bus, with timetable information at www.vitagroup.it.

For Valsesia and access to Alagna, buses operated by Baranzelli have a direct connection from Milan via Novara to Alagna. Tickets are available on the bus, with timetable information at www.baranzelli.it. To reach Macugnaga and the Valle Anzasca, buses are operated by Comazzi with a direct route to Macugnaga from Domodossola. Domodossola can be reached by train (from both Italian and Swiss stations), and by bus. Tickets are available on the bus, and timetables at www.comazzibus.com.

By car

In Italy, the main valleys do have car parking available, but the options are standard parking spaces; not like the secure parking structures in Switzerland. Leaving your car is at your own risk. Access to the valleys is broadly directed on the Italian Autostrada network (toll roads) via Turin and Milan, towards the Aosta

GETTING AROUND BETWEEN VALLEYS ON THE TMR

You can make the best possible plans for a trek, but when conditions on the trail or with your party change, then plans have to adapt. It's not especially easy to move between the valley centres around the TMR due to the challenging geography.

To get from Switzerland to Italy, the fastest option is to take the cable car from Zermatt to Breuil-Cervinia. If the weather forces a closure, then the only option is a long journey.

For access from Switzerland to the eastern Italian valleys:

- Train (or bus from Saastal) to Visp or Brig (SBB)
- From Visp or Brig, train to Domodossola (SBB)
- For access to Valle Anzasca, bus from Domodossola to Macugnaga (Comazzi)
- Train from Domodossola to Novara (TrenItalia)
- For access to Valsesia, bus from Novara to Alagna (Baranzelli)

From Switzerland to the western (Valle d'Aosta) Italian valleys:

- Train (or bus from Saastal) to Visp (SBB)
- Train from Visp to Martigny (SBB)
- Bus from Martigny to Aosta (Transports de Martigny et Régions SA (TMR))
- Bus from Aosta to Val d'Ayas via Verrès, or to Gressoney/Stafal via Pont-Saint-Martin (V.I.T.A.)

Access between the Mattertal and Saastal in Switzerland is through the PostBus network, and SBB trains along the Mattertal.

Access between the Italian valleys requires a lengthy trip by regional bus, or it is possible to travel between the Valle del Lys (Gressoney valley) and Valsesia (Alagna) by cable car.

Valley (E25) and the connections to the Valle d'Ayas and Gressoney valley; or towards Domodossola (E62) and the connection to Valle Anzasca (Macugnaga).

WEATHER

With the Monte Rosa massif forming such an immense barrier between Switzerland and Italy and the deep valleys branching from the mountain chain, the climate can vary enormously depending on where you are and at what altitude. In general, the Swiss side of the route experiences less rainfall – in the shadow of the mountain wall that borders Italy – with the rain and snow that does occur often focusing on the mountain tops. Snow can fall throughout the year, and it is not unknown for a summer heatwave to be followed within days by sustained snowfall, even down in the valley bottom. Average high temperatures in the summer months in Zermatt range between 15° and 20°C, with an average of 185mm of rain in the month (June and August likely to have more rainfall) (source: weather-and-climate.com).

In Italy, the geography of the valleys, which spread like outstretched fingers from Monte Rosa, have resulted in different climate conditions. The valleys are between 30 to 50km long, stretching generally southwards towards the Po valley. Warm, damp air from the plain and Mediterranean is funnelled up the valleys before meeting the icy walls of the Monte Rosa massif, rising,

The stunning view from Gandegghütte is dominated by the Breithorn (right), with Liskamm and Monte Rosa beyond (Stages 1/2)

cooling, and forming precipitation. Consequently, the upper Italian valleys are greener, a little cooler, and prone to forming cloud in the afternoons with rain and thunderstorms. The chances are good, however, that this will clear for mountain views in the morning. Average high temperatures in Macugnaga range from 14° to 20°C in the summer months, cooling overnight with average lows around 6°C, with rainfall averaging 240mm per month (source: weather-and-climate.com).

The higher the altitude, the cooler the temperature. Depending on humidity and pressure, for every 100m of altitude, the temperature could cool 0.65°C. This means that a high pass could be 10° colder than the valley.

Weather in the mountains can be unpredictable and dangerous. You may have very little warning before a storm could roll in over the mountains. Thunderstorms are most common in August, but strong winds, rain, and snow can happen at any time. If you are caught in a storm; find shelter as soon as you can and/or descend as quickly and safely as you can. In a thunderstorm, you may need to abandon your trekking poles and other potential lightning conductors.

For the latest weather forecasts from weather stations at different altitudes, www.mountain-forecast.com provides a good range of information including cloud base, snow and precipitation information, wind chill and freezing level. MeteoSwiss also provides an excellent service for Switzerland, with both app and online information at www.meteoswiss.admin.ch.

FOOD

Swiss Valaisian food is rooted in its pastoral, mountain history, and involves plenty of meat, potatoes, bread, and cheese. In the Swiss towns, there are far more choices, but when staying in a mountain hut in Switzerland or Italy, you can expect a four-course dinner generally involving a combination of soup, salad, pasta, stew or main course, and a dessert. Breakfasts in huts offer a simple selection of bread with jam, as well as fruit, muesli, yoghurt, and tea or coffee.

In Italy, the mountainous regions and Walser migrations result in similar local cuisine, with the addition of more polenta and pasta. *Pasta alla Macugnaghese* is an excellent example of this fusion, as it combines pasta with a sauce of potatoes, toma cheese, butter and bacon. It will certainly give you plenty of energy!

For lunch and refreshments along the way, huts will be able to offer drinks and usually an option of cakes and strudels throughout the day, or a more substantial lunchtime meal. Many huts may be able to provide a packed lunch for the following day – you will need to ask about this before or as you arrive. Alternatively, grocery shops have been identified in the Stage facilities planner and on the stage maps, so you can plan your resupplies.

There have been enormous improvements in catering for those with dietary requirements, but do bear in mind that mountain huts have limited supplies and will need to plan ahead; they will appreciate an early warning. The exception is the Oresteshütte (variant for Stages 3/4), which is entirely vegan.

Remember that if you are staying at a high-altitude hut around 3000m, like the Britanniahütte or Rifugio del Teodulo, then they have extremely limited water supplies, and you will need to buy bottled water (at quite a cost).

MONEY

Italy uses the Euro (€), while Switzerland has the Swiss Franc (CHF). Nearly all shops, restaurants and mountain huts can take card payments, but in case there are power issues or they don't, then take enough cash to cover your costs. There are a number of banks and ATMs along the TMR route; these have been identified on the Stage facilities planner and maps for quick reference.

LANGUAGES

Throughout the TMR, English is widely understood, but it is always worth learning a few key words and phrases; it will be appreciated for visits to mountain huts, restaurants and shops, and when you are emailing huts to book accommodation. While Switzerland has four official languages, the Mattertal and Saastal use Swiss German (*Schweizerdeutsch*). The typical mountain greeting used between hikers is *Grüezi* (an abbreviation of *Gott grüez-i*, meaning 'may God greet you').

In Italy, the unique history of the upper valleys has resulted in quite a range of acceptable languages. Italian is the first choice, but you can also find French widely used in the Valle d'Ayas, and German (Walser German) used in the Gressoney, Valsesia and Anzasca valleys. Gressoney – or the Valle del Lys – has street signs in both Italian and German, alluding to the impact of its Walser cultural past. Hiking in Italy, the typical mountain greeting is either *buongiorno* or *salve*.

WAYMARKS AND ROUTE FINDING

The TMR is an established route, but the frequency of 'TMR' signage can vary; it is more likely that signposts will direct you towards the next pass or village. There are a number of small metal plaques that attach to signposts and show the entire TMR route but these are infrequent. Wayfinding is generally very good along the TMR: with signposts at path junctions and painted markers on rocks and trees along the paths. However, it is important to pay close attention when there are difficult areas; such as among moraine and boulder fields, when there is snow cover (which covers painted markers on rocks), or when visibility is poor. In such conditions, take care, keep looking, and be prepared to double-back if it looks like you've gone wrong.

In Italy, you are far more likely to see 'TMR' emblazoned on rocks and on signposts. Italian walking signposts are in yellow or white, and the TMR will be indicated instead of the local path number, along with a difficulty rating (T refers to an easy walking trail, E to a harder hiking trail, and EE to a more technical hiking route, potentially with very steep areas or scrambling). Painted waymarks can vary, and tend to involve red or yellow arrows, potentially with 'TMR' also painted.

In Switzerland, most signposts are also yellow, and have difficulty ratings. Low-level and gentle walking routes are indicated with yellow (yellow diamonds on trees and rock waymarks), while mountain hiking routes have a red and white stripe on signposts, and for paint waymarks. Switzerland also has blue signposts and blue-and-white paint waymarks for technical Alpine routes.

The Swiss do not tend to use 'TMR' as an official sign in the same way as Italy. Their own 'Swiss Tour of Monte Rosa' is the section of the TMR between Saas-Fee and Zermatt, and is signed as Swiss Route 27 (in green). The Europaweg is a part of this, but *also* has its own signage as well.

MAPS AND APPS

The stages in this guide use 1:100,000 maps to provide a sense of the route, the altitude and the facilities on the way. They use OpenData and have been thoroughly checked for accuracy and amended with key features of the trail.

Most hikers rely on map apps for on-trail navigation, preferring that to carrying separate maps. You must, therefore, be confident that your phone battery can be relied upon. All the huts along the TMR have sockets for charging, but some huts have very limited socket numbers.

SwissMobility has both a website and app version for their excellent maps, onto which hiking trails (and more crucially, trail closures) can be viewed at https://map.schweizmobil.ch, but this only covers the Swiss side of the trail. It is nevertheless an excellent site to check, particularly given the Europaweg's tendency to have closed sections.

Alternatives like OutdoorActive, Gaia GPS, and HiiKER provide (often for a subscription fee) a variety of different underlying maps to use, with the TMR as a recognised route to follow.

Varied waymarks on the TMR (clockwise from top right): TMR plaque, Europaweg plaque, painted TMR and Turlo waymarks in Italy, rockfall warning on the Europaweg, Swiss signage for Route 27

Europaweg Grächen-Zermatt
Europahütte 1 h 25
Zermatt 8 h
Zermatt
1 h
2 h 35
5 h 15
27
27
TMR
Monte Moro
Macugnaga
Alagna
Gressoney
St. Jacques
Theodul
Zermatt
Grächen
Saas Fee
Monte Moro
EUROPAWEG
GRÄCHEN-ZERMATT
C.A.I. SEZ. VARALLO
RIF. BARBA-FERRERO
-H.1,45
CAP. RESEGOTTI
207 -H.5,00
COLLE DEL TURLO
207F-207A H.3,00
TMR

If you prefer paper sheet maps, the best options are:

- Swisstopo 105 Valais/Wallis, 1:100,000 (covers the whole TMR area)
- Swisstopo 5006 Matterhorn Mischabel, 1:50,000 (covers the whole Swiss side)
- Swisstopo 3306T Zermatt–Saas-Fee–Matterhorn hiking map, 1:30,000 (covers sections in Switzerland around Zermatt and Saas-Fee)
- Kompass 87 Breuil-Cervinia, Zermatt, 1:50,000 (covers Zermatt to the Gressoney valley, Stages 1 to 3)
- Kompass 88 Monte Rosa, Valle Anzasca, Valsesia, 1:50,000 (covers most of the Italian valleys, Stages 3 to 8)
- IGC 108 Cervinio Matterhorn 1:25,000 (covers Zermatt to the Valle d'Ayas, Stages 1 and 2)
- IGC 109 Monte Rosa 1:25,000 (covers Gressoney/Stafal to the Passo Monte Moro, Stages 3 to 6)

SAFETY IN THE MOUNTAINS

Most hikers complete their TMR without mishap. Part of having a successful trip is understanding and planning for the potential dangers associated with an Alpine trek. As the TMR goes to high and wild places, the risks associated with being caught in difficult terrain or having an accident can be serious.

Fitness and preparation

Make sure that you are fit and healthy enough for the trek, and that you can walk throughout the day in your boots and pack without pain. People within a group will have different preferences and walking speeds; use the information in this guide to plan out an itinerary that gives you enough time for walking, breaks, and reaching your next shelter before nightfall.

Weather

The main factor influencing your safety on the TMR may be the weather. Make sure you take the right equipment, as you may encounter storms, snow, rain, below-freezing temperatures, and heatwaves. In thunderstorms, avoid climbing higher or onto exposed terrain like ridges. Leave your poles and find shelter as soon as you can (but avoid lone trees, caves, gullies or overhanging rocks). If the weather is really foul, you may need to wait a day or longer for the conditions to improve.

Trail conditions

Depending on when you walk the TMR, conditions on the trail may be very different. Snow will likely be very prevalent in the early season, particularly over high passes. Microspikes and poles can make an enormous difference in such conditions. Take care on sections of the walk that cross old snow; it will be melting and unstable.

Sections of the TMR can go through very loose and treacherous

The narrow path clings and scrambles along the sheer slopes (Stage 9)

terrain that is prone to rockfalls. This is especially prevalent on the Europaweg in the Mattertal; a route that often will have closed sections. There are instructions along more dangerous routes that advise to move through rockfall areas quickly or direct you towards reinforced zones. If any of the sections on the TMR are closed, there will be alternative options to your next stop, though this may require a longer walk, or dropping into the valley. For the latest information on path closures, see https://map.schweizmobil.ch. Or contact the guardians at the local mountain huts for their advice.

Accidents and mountain rescue

In case of an accident, firstly, stay calm and assess the situation for your safety. If it is safe to do so for the affected person, move them and yourself away from any hazards (eg. rockfalls, avalanche) and apply immediate first aid. Keep them warm, using any spare clothing (and an emergency bivi sack if you have one). Make a note of your exact location (the emergency app echoSOS is worthwhile and can both contact and provide emergency services with your location), and contact a mountain hut if nearby, or the mountain rescue.

- Switzerland: call 144 or 112
- Italy: call 118 or 112

If you cannot go for help, the international distress signal (see the front of this book) is six blasts on a whistle every 10 seconds in one minute, or, if dark, six flashes of a torch, followed by a minute's pause. Repeat as long as required. The response to this signal is for three whistles or torch flashes through a minute (one every

20 seconds), followed by a minute's pause.

Insurance

Mountain rescue is expensive, so make sure you have adequate insurance that covers it; this will likely require a specialist insurer such as the BMC (British Mountaineering Council), Austrian Alpine Club, Snowcard Insurance or DogTag Travel Insurance (see Appendix B). You should also ensure that you have medical insurance cover. EU and UK citizens should carry their EHIC or GHIC (European/Global Health Insurance Card) which provides access to medically necessary, state-provided health care while you're abroad.

GLACIER CROSSING

The TMR may be the first introduction to glacier walking for many hikers. The Theodulgletscher (Stage 2), Allalingletscher and Hohlaubgletscher (Stage 7) are among the most 'user friendly' glaciers you can encounter with established routes to follow, but the inherently unstable and changing nature of glaciers means that great conditions cannot be guaranteed. It is important to evaluate whether you are suitably prepared and equipped before crossing any glaciers, and that the conditions of the ice are safe enough.

For information on walking the TMR without the glacier crossings, see 'Route and schedule options'.

Wet or dry glacier? A wet glacier is the more dangerous option and describes when a glacier is covered in snow and hikers cannot see holes and crevasses. In those conditions, full glacier gear is essential.

Dangers

The main danger on glaciers are crevasses and holes in the ice. All glaciers have them, and the conditions can (and will) change year on year, especially given the unprecedented shrinking of the alpine glaciers. Crevasse rescue, when one of your party has fallen in a crevasse, is a key skill in mountaineering, but assumes that you will be roped up with the right equipment to self-rescue or be hoisted out. The other risks concern the steepness of the glacier and the consequences of a slip, rockfall from mountains above the glacier, and the challenges of dealing with poor visibility and 'white-outs' when on a glacier, which can be incredibly disorientating, making it very easy to stray off the route and into dangerous territory.

On the Theodulgletscher, most of the route follows an established, pisted ice track that is built of compacted ice on top of the glacier and used by ski and maintenance vehicles, so the risk of crevasses is small, and generally located at the edges of the glacier. The only steep section is the climb up a snow/ice slope between

Crossing the Allalingletscher (Stage 7)

the glacier and the Theodulpass. There is occasional, minor stone fall from the nearby Theodulhorn to keep an eye on.

On the Allalingletscher and Hohlaubgletscher, there are glacial streams and more crevasses near the route, which follows a path that picks its way across the ice and over medial moraines. Do not diverge from this route. The walking is not steep, but the ice at the edge of the glaciers can be steep and fragile.

If you do find yourself needing rescue; call for mountain rescue on 144 (Swiss emergency number) or 112 (European emergency number). Ensure that you have adequate insurance, such as that from the Austrian Alpine Club, BMC or another organisation (see Appendix B).

Guides

If you have never walked on a glacier before and have not used crampons or microspikes, you should get some experience with a professional instructor. You can either do this before your TMR, or hire a mountain guide to assist in your crossing of the Theodulgletscher on your trek. Zermatters is where you can go to hire a guide; they have a centre at Bahnhofstrasse 58 in Zermatt, and information online at www.zermatters.ch/en. Ask about their 'Easy Guided Glacier Tour' for a first experience, or their 'Monte Rosa Tour – Theodul Glacier Crossing' for guiding during the trek.

If you are a novice with glaciers, the high route (Stages 7 and 8) via Britanniahütte is best avoided,

From the Theodulpass, looking back to the Theodulgletscher and the Mischabel range (Stage 2)

and hikers should take Stage 7A, the lower-level, official route.

Equipment

If you are confident about crossing glaciers, then you will need to take crampons or microspikes. Full-fledged glacier travel also requires rope, harnesses and other mountaineering equipment and is recommended for when conditions are more challenging (eg early in the season), but for the TMR's small amount of time on well-travelled glaciers (in appropriate conditions), traction support is the most critical.

Conditions

Plan to cross early in the day where possible, so the ice is at its most solid. For crossing the Theodulgletscher, this means staying at Gandegghütte for the anti-clockwise route, or Rif del Teodulo for the opposite direction. The best conditions to look for are for a 'dry' glacier; meaning that the ice is not covered in snow. Snow cover means that holes and crevasses in the ice are hard to spot, and that the established crossing routes may be harder to find. The guardians at nearby mountain huts will be able to advise you on the latest glacier conditions and if they are safe for hikers.

If you are facing poor conditions – new snow, poor visibility, storms – then you will need to evaluate whether you are prepared and safe for glacier walking, as more mountaineering equipment including a rope would be advisable. The TMR is lucky to have alternative options available; if you are unsure, then do not place yourself at risk and take an alternative route or stay put until conditions to improve.

THE MONTE ROSA REGION

Monte Rosa's east face, from left: Signalkuppe, Zumsteinspitze, Dufourspitze, Nordend

HISTORY AND CULTURE

The long span of human history in the Alps has encompassed era-defining events, from Hannibal's crossing of the Alps, to the rise of the Roman Empire, the long reach and control of the Church and the Duchy of Savoy, Napolean's invasion of Italy, and the creation of the Swiss Confederation. The Alps are an obstacle, a crossing point, a lifeline of trade and migration. But the history of the Monte Rosa region is far from the grand armies of invasion and battles over territory. This is a quieter, isolated history, of generations of lives spent in the meadows and villages under the towering peaks, of tradition, farming, and claiming the rugged and inhospitable land for their own. For all that the Passo Monte Moro and Theodulpass have their place among the key cross-border routes over the Alps, they never claimed the same level of importance as the Grand and Petit St Bernard, or the Simplonpass to the east. The notes on the history of the Monte Rosa region below are a brief summary of the ebb and flow of the controlling powers; more information on local history is included in information boxes in the each TMR stage.

As is the case with many areas of Europe, historical records invariably begin with the Romans. Their founding of Aosta (Augusta Praetoria Salassorum) and conquest of the Aosta valleys from the incumbent Salassi tribe took over 100 years before Roman victory. As the Empire expanded northwards into the Valais region and Germany, evidence of Roman coins in the high reaches of the pass suggest the use of Valle Tournanche and Valle d'Ayas to access the Theodulpass and Rhône Valley from Aosta.

With the decline of Rome, control over land splintered between lords, regional powers and the distant hand of the Holy Roman Empire, beginning with the Burgundians. The pervasive power that united the region was the Church, which itself claimed large swathes of land under the aegis of the Bishopric of Sion and its monasteries. While nominally the sovereign power of the Valais, the Prince-Bishop of Sion was obliged to cede secular power to the Seven Tithings (*Sieben Zenden*); medieval communes in the Upper Valais (including the Mattertal and Saastal), which enjoyed particular privileges granted by the Holy Roman Emperor in 1353. By 1613, the Seven Tithings formally declared their independence from the Bishopric and became the Republic of the Seven Tithings, an associate and ally – but not a canton – of the Old Swiss Confederacy.

In Italy, the Counts and Dukes of Savoy – also subject to the Holy Roman Empire – held control over the Aostan valleys from 1031 before evolving into the Kingdom of Sicily in 1720. Aside from a handful of

Historic alpine life on a mural at Rif Gabiet (Stages 3/4)

periods under French control, the lands remained under Savoy control – with certain communes granted considerable autonomy – up until the invasion of Italy by Napoleon. The eastern Italian valleys in the Monte Rosa region spent some time in Savoy, and other times were controlled by the Duchy of Milan.

The Seven Tithings and control of the Italian dukes came to an end with the French Revolution and subsequent invasion by Napoleon. The Valais briefly became part of the Helvetic Republic, before becoming part of the French Empire. From 1815 and Napoleon's defeat, it became fully part of the revived Swiss Confederation.

For Italy, after Napoleon, the Kingdom of Sardinia was restored until the unification of Italy in 1861, while the Duchy of Milan instead became part of the Kingdom of Lombardy-Venetia, a constituent of the Austrian Empire, until it was annexed into the Kingdom of Italy in 1866.

Between Napoleon's time and the breakout of WW1, the economic horizons of the Monte Rosa region changed substantially for the first time, with income from farming and mining supplemented by tourism, as a result of the improved transport connections (particularly in Switzerland, with the establishment of its railways). Visiting the Alps became popular for wealthy travellers on their Grand Tours, as well as opening the door to aspiring alpinists (see the 'Golden Age of Mountaineering' below). With visitors came opportunities and wealth; hotels sprang up among the villages, local people became guides to the visitors seeking the best views or routes into the mountains, and improved roads and rail brought new connections to isolated communities.

The two World Wars did not overly impact the region; Switzerland remained neutral throughout both, while most fighting for Italy took place on its eastern mountainous borders with Austria in WW1, and across the Mediterranean and in Italy itself in WW2.

THE WALSER

The name Walser, from *Wallis* (German) or *Valais* (French), describes the people who settled throughout the Monte Rosa region. The Walser are essentially a people connected by language – in this case, dialects

Walser-style buildings at Rif Pastore in Valsesia (Stages 4/5)

of Highest Alemannic – and cultural tradition. Alemannic refers to the *allemani* (meaning 'all men'); a confederation of Germanic tribes first mentioned by Roman authors in the third century AD, some of whom subsequently migrated south into the Alps. As the name and language suggests, the Walser's origins are from Germany and Switzerland, and records have traced their further expansion south to settle in the high Italian valleys in multiple migrations in the 12th and 13th centuries. Reasons for these migrations remain speculative, but theories refer to: natural expansion, as people searched for better land given the more arid climate on the Swiss side; opportunity, given the passes were clear of glaciers at the time; encouraged migration, as alliances and ownership of the land changed hands, with tenants encouraged to move and settle elsewhere; and avoidance of feudal lords in the valleys.

Because the lands the Walser settled in were inhospitable and isolated, the incoming settlers were often welcomed in establishing their farming colonies; having people occupying these high alpine regions meant trade, protection of the passes, and stewardship of the land. In recognition and support of this, local lords would confer special rights and independence on their Walser settlers and in turn benefited from the extra population and commerce. Each valley where the Walser settled has its own history; this is explored to a further extent in the information boxes in each stage.

The Walser way of life was fundamentally one of transhumance farming, of living in connection to the cycle of seasons. Winter would be spent in the clustered villages in the valleys along with the livestock. In spring, as the snows melted, grazing would return to the valley meadows, before families would travel into the high pastures for the summer, living and working with the herd in scattered lodgings. The high *alpe* buildings that can still be found along the TMR are testament to those summer homes. Even today, the descent of herds at the end of summer back to the valleys is a time-honoured celebration of a successful season.

The aptitude and adaptation to the mountains is the other hallmark of Walser people and the regions they chose to settle; the passes encountered on the TMR were all key connections between these isolated communities, and were the main routes for migration and trade. In most cases, the remnants of paved, pack-horse tracks that wind through forests and into the high reaches of the mountains to the passes exist because of the Walser, who clearly built both houses and roads to last.

This remains a living cultural identity, and current Walser people are justifiably proud of the resilience and mountain traditions of their forebears. Every three years, Walser from around the world meet for the

Walsertreffen, a festival or meeting of Walser people and celebration of the culture. To learn more about the Walser and to explore examples of their historic homes, Alagna (Stage 4) and Macugnaga (Stage 5/6) both have Walser museums, as does Gressoney (Stage 3, off-route).

MONTE ROSA AND THE GOLDEN AGE OF MOUNTAINEERING

The Golden Age of Mountaineering was the decade between 1854 and 1865 during which the first ascents of most of the great mountains in the Alps took place. This doesn't include Mont Blanc, however, as that ascent was initiated by the renowned Alpine writer and naturalist Horace-Bénédict de Saussure, and first climbed by Jacques Balmat and Michel Paccard in 1786.

The golden decade began with ascents on Monte Rosa and culminated with the ascent and tragedy of Edward Whymper's expedition on the Matterhorn (see Stage 1), making the Monte Rosa region pivotal to the early alpinists. The period was dominated by British climbers and their Swiss and French guides. This was a time when science and sport were interlinked, and records in the *Alpine Journal* from the time eagerly document experiments in the high Alps as often as expeditions. Others too, from artists to poets were attracted to the buzz and adventure of alpine exploration, with eminent artists such as John Ruskin and William Wordsworth venturing into the valleys, if not up the peaks.

Trekkers take in the enormous flank of the Weisshorn, on the final approach to Europahütte (Stage 10)

Attempts to climb Monte Rosa – and to discover her highest peak – started in earnest from the Italian valleys in 1778 with a group of Italian climbers seeking a lost valley among the glaciers. Attempts quickly followed by the Count of Morzzo of Turin, and by de Saussure. The first success on a Monte Rosa summit came in 1819 by two men of Gressoney – Johann Niklaus and Joseph Vincent – who reached the top of Piramide Vincent. They next found success the following year on the Zumsteinspitze, accompanied by Joseph Zumstein. It took another 22 years before Alagna's parish priest, Giovanni Gnifetti, climbed Punta Gnifetti (or Signalkuppe) in 1842. It must have been gruelling for these early adventurers to reach such incredible heights for the first time, only to realise that Monte Rosa still had higher summits they'd yet to reach.

Finally, on 1 August 1855, Monte Rosa's highest peak – Dufourspitze – was summited from Zermatt by a group comprising Charles Hudson, John Birkbeck, Edward Stephenson, James and Christopher Smyth, and their guides Ulrich Lauener and Johannes and Matthäus Zumtaugwald. It wasn't until 1872, however, that the first successful ascent of Monte Rosa from Macugnaga was achieved, via the massive east face.

Perhaps one of the most accomplished early climbers was Lucy Walker, who claimed the first female ascent of Monte Rosa in 1862 with her guide, Melchior Anderegg. The most renowned female alpinist of the time, she holds the title for the first female ascent of 16 alpine summits, including the Matterhorn, the Strahlhorn and the Eiger. Next time you take in the view of Monte Rosa, the Matterhorn, the Rimpfischhorn, the Dom and the Weisshorn – imagine climbing them in a dress!

The allure of climbing Monte Rosa continued through the 20th and into the 21st centuries. Winston Churchill made a successful ascent in 1894 (not only was Monte Rosa higher, but the

HISTORIC TOURS OF MONTE ROSA

The Tour of Monte Rosa is not a new trail – quite the opposite! While the specific route may have adapted over the years, the idea of a circuit around Monte Rosa has caught the imagination of many travellers over the past couple of centuries (and perhaps longer, given the well-trodden migratory and trade routes). Accounts of and guides to the route are surprisingly prolific, and range from grand scientific works on the geology, glaciation and plant life of the Alps, including Horace Bénédict de Saussure's *Voyages dans les Alps*, to travelogues from 18th and 19th century travellers and climbers. Appendix C – Further reading includes a few examples of these accounts.

guide fees were apparently cheaper than for the Matterhorn at the time). In recent times, climbers have been attracted by the Spaghetti Tour, an epic multi-day traverse of the ridge and peaks of the Monte Rosa massif, including the Breithorn, Pollox, Castor, Liskamm, Piramide Vincent, and the core Monte Rosa summits.

GEOLOGY

The Alps are, as mountain ranges go, relatively young, forming between 40 and 25 million years ago. The tectonic plates underpinning the continents of Africa and Europe collided, as the African plate pushed northwards and up while the European plate folded beneath, and the land that had existed between them was caught in the middle. In parts of the Alps, the visual representation of layers of rock being folded like fabric can be clearly seen – strata of different rock types painting the mountains in striped shades. The Monte Rosa massif constitutes a nappe (a nappe typically forms at a tectonic boundary, when a great mass of rock is forced over a different plane of rock and moved from its original place), made up of crystalline basement rock – meaning that the metamorphic rock of the massif is particularly ancient, as it was once just above the mantle, under all other rocks and sediments before the plate collision forced Monte Rosa to form.

Tectonics only form part of the story of the Alpine geology; glaciation was the next tool to carve new shapes into the landscape. Since the last ice age, glaciers have gone through phases of shrinking (such as in the Middle Ages, where accounts suggest the Theodulpass was ice-free), and growing (such as during the Little Ice Age, where by the 18th century glaciers reached their greatest extent in recent times). Glaciers carved the great U-shaped valleys surrounding Monte Rosa, with hanging valleys forming where the pressure of the ice from subsidiary glaciers wore through the rock at a slower pace to the larger glaciers, leaving a sharp drop where the smaller valley now meets the deep trough of the larger.

The shrinking of the alpine glaciers from the current warming climate has left long stretches of bare and polished rock, and great fields of moraine. The speed of the shrinking continues to be fast, and results in unstable and often changing landscapes. This can often be seen on the TMR with swollen streams and unstable boulder fields and moraine. The rock itself, usually granite gneiss and schist, is often friable, and the relentless millennia of freeze–thaw erosion and glaciation has left the core substance of the mountains prone to fractures.

WILDLIFE AND FLOWERS

Animals

It is a common delight along the TMR to be accompanied not only by

A curious ibex caught in the rising sun above Gandegghütte (Stage 2)

the grandeur of the mountains, but also by the sound and sight of local wildlife. Eagles and alpine choughs (black, red legs, yellow bill) dominate the air, even at high altitude, and the tiny alpine wall creeper (greyish body, with vivid splashes of red wings) is a particularly memorable find.

Among the high pastures, you will often hear marmots before you see them. A high-pitched whistle of a call acts as an alert for the marmot madness (the collective noun for marmots) to be wary of dangers. Marmots are among the largest of rodents; they live in colonies in burrows, and spend the summer months fattening up, eating grasses and insects before hibernating for the winter.

Ibex are also a regular sight on the TMR. They differentiate from their smaller chamois cousins with longer, thicker horns, and larger bodies. Like chamois (smaller, with more delicate, highly-curved horns, and a white blaze down the face), they generally live in herds in the high reaches of the Alps between the treeline and the snows and are incredibly agile. Expect to see ibex on the more remote passes, like the Colle d'Olen and Turlo, and potentially grazing near high huts in the evenings.

Wolves and lynx have been reintroduced after being hunted to extinction by the early 20th century. There are known wolf packs throughout the Alps, but sightings are very rare, and it is highly unlikely that you will spot these elusive predators.

Opposite: A wide variety of wild alpine flowers on the TMR

While not *wild*life, the TMR often will travel through areas with livestock roaming their summer pastures. Sheep, goats and cows should all be expected along the route where the toll of bells ought to give you fair warning. Remember to keep your distance where practical. Also keep an eye out for signs and warnings that herds may be accompanied by a *patou* – a shepherd dog that lives with the herd and who takes their job to protect the flock very seriously; particularly relevant given the reintroduction of wolves. They may look like giant golden retrievers, but do not approach a *patou*, and if they investigate you, stay calm, stay away from their herd, and avoid any behaviour that could be seen as confrontational.

Plants

The plant life around Monte Rosa is highly varied, due in part to the difference in rainfall between the Italian and Swiss valleys. The Italian valleys are far more lush, but on both sides, typical Alpine vegetation prevails, with mixed forests of spruce, pine and larch (the latter is a deciduous conifer, and covers the valley slopes gold in autumn) on the lower slopes, giving way to rugged and rocky grassy hillsides, and finally to bare rock and snow. Even at the higher altitudes however, among the most barren scree slopes, alpine flowers can be found like tiny jewels among the rocks.

Only hardy plants can thrive in the high reaches of the Alps as they spend a fair proportion of the year covered in snow. As the snows retreat, the meadows spring back into life in a flurry of colour as delicate and resilient flowers cover the hillsides. Given that the TMR often climbs high and snows can linger into late summer, 'spring' can come to those hillsides throughout the walking season, and your TMR is likely to feature displays of flowers along the way. For more information, Gillian Price's invaluable mini-guide *Alpine Flowers* (Cicerone Press) gives information on 230 varieties of flower, all searchable by colour.

THE TOUR OF MONTE ROSA

The vast east face of Monte Rosa from Rif Oberto Maroli, the largest mountain wall in the Alps (Stages 6/7)

STAGE 1

Zermatt to Gandegghütte

Start	Zermatt (1616m)
Finish	Gandegghütte (3028m)
Walking time	4hr 10min
Distance	10.5km
Ascent	1450m
Descent	35m
High point	Gandegghütte (3028m)
Variant	Options to bypass Furi and Trockener Steg

There is no particularly gentle way to start the TMR. This first stage is overwhelmingly uphill, climbing from Zermatt to over 3000m. But what the stage lacks in a gradual introduction, it more than makes up for in the spectacular views and high alpine splendour of the peaks surrounding Zermatt.

On no other stage of the TMR (nor on many other walks in the Alps) can you expect to be surrounded by so many 4000m giants. The summits emerge as you climb, one after another, as the bustle of Zermatt gives way to dappled forests, alpine pastures, and finally bare rock and glaciers. Gandegghütte is in a spectacular spot, tucked beneath the monumental Breithorn to the east, and the Matterhorn to the west.

The cable car from Zermatt can be used to reach Furi and Trockener Steg (and, if you are skipping the glacier crossing, the cable car can take you all the way into Italy). But on a clear day the alpine scenery and excellent walk shouldn't be missed. A day or two spent acclimatising before you start the trek is highly recommended.

ZERMATT

Zermatt is one of the world's most iconic mountain towns, and every year thousands of visitors step off the train; pilgrims to the greatest concentration of 4000m summits in the Alps, with the incomparable view of the Matterhorn overhead. Whether visitors to Zermatt are here to climb, trek, bike or use any of the myriad options to whisk people higher and closer to the mountains than they may have experienced before, the goal is simple: Alpine splendour and Valaisian hospitality.

Long before tourism became the lifeblood of the town, and the Gornergrat railway winched up the northern slopes of Riffelberg, Zermatt and its surrounding villages were home to some of the earliest established settlements in Switzerland. Small timber barns in Z'mutt for instance, date back to the 1100s. Perhaps due to its relative isolation, the inhabitants of Zermatt have always had an unusual amount of independence; even in the 13th century, when Zermatt was under the authority of the Bishop of Sion, residents had their own rights over land and freedoms for administration. In the 16th century, those rights consolidated, as groups of families bought their freedom from rule and tithing rights and formed their own municipality and farmers' guild within the borders of the Republic of the Seven Tithings.

Zermatt was broadly self-sufficient in its challenging terrain and climate; a small farming village in the high Valais, with occasional migrants and trade (including in salt) passing over the Theodulpass into Italy. From the mid-nineteenth century, the establishment of railways and easier travel into the Alps meant that more and more visitors started 'discovering' Zermatt and its peaks. This was the golden age of mountaineering, and while early visitors laboured up the long and winding track from Visp, by 1891, the Visp–Zermatt railway had been constructed, and only seven years later in 1898, the Gornergrat Bahn (the first electric rack railway in Switzerland, and the second such in the world), began operating. Zermatt was transformed.

As much as Zermatt has done to promote travel and tourism, it has done so with thoughts of safeguarding itself; no cars are allowed in the town (they must be parked down the valley in Täsch), the town is committed to sustainability and energy self-sufficiency, and even new buildings retain a traditional Valaisian style. Zermatt today has every amenity a visitor could want – if they have a deep enough wallet. With excellent train connections, and unmatched hiking and exploring available, Zermatt is the most convenient destination for travellers and for a few days of acclimatising before you start your trek; and the most iconic town to celebrate your finish.

Note: between Zermatt and Stafal (Stage 3) there are few facilities, remember to stock up in Zermatt, or arrange for packed lunches at your accommodation.

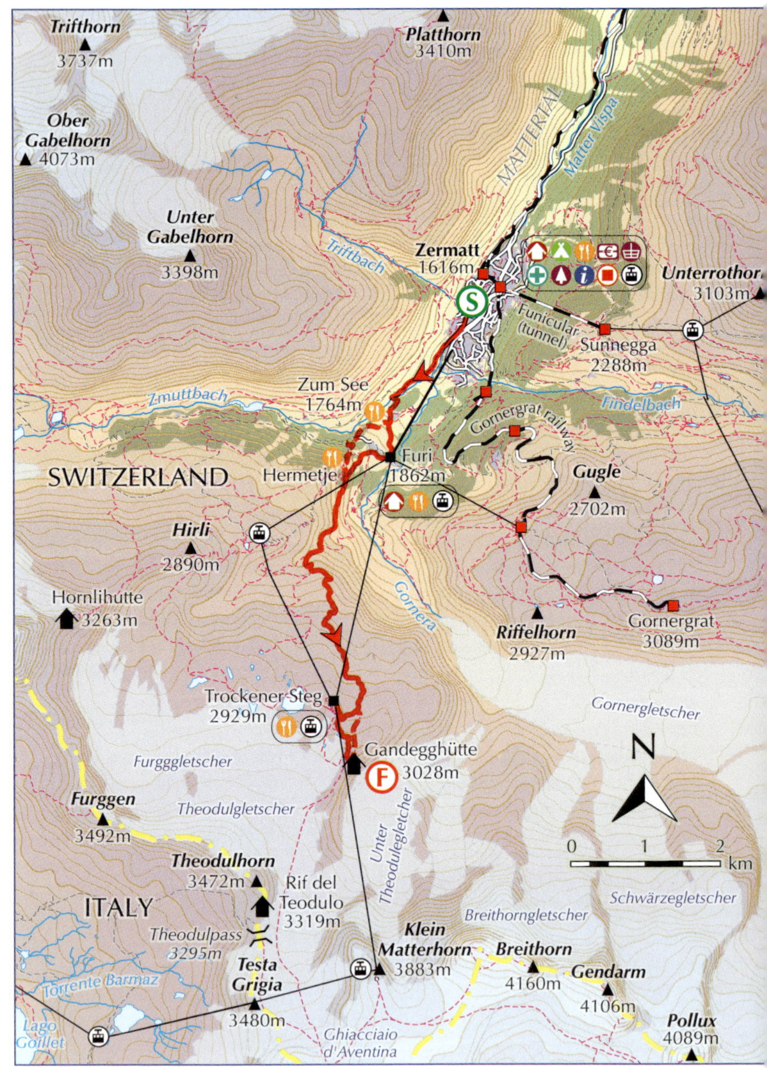
Trifthorn
3737m
Platthorn
3410m
Ober
Gabelhorn
4073m
MATTERTAL
Matter Vispa
Unter
Gabelhorn
3398m
Triftbach
Zermatt
1616m
Unterrothorn
3103m
Funicular
(tunnel)
Sunnegga
2288m
Zum See
1764m
Zmuttbach
Findelbach
Gornergrat railway
Furi
1862m
Hermetje
SWITZERLAND
Gugle
2702m
Hirli
2890m
Hornlihütte
3263m
Gornera
Riffelhorn
2927m
Gornergrat
3089m
Gornergletscher
Trockener Steg
2929m
Gandegghütte
3028m
Furgggletscher
N
Furggen
3492m
Theodulgletscher
Unter
Theodulegletscher
0
1
2
km
Theodulhorn
3472m
Rif del
Teodulo
3319m
ITALY
Schwärzegletscher
Breithorngletscher
Theodulpass
3295m
Klein
Matterhorn
3883m
Breithorn
4160m
Gendarm
4106m
Testa
Grigia
3480m
Torrente Barmaz
Lago
Goillet
Ghiacciaio
d'Aventina
Pollux
4089m

Facilities Stage 1			
0hr		Zermatt	cable car available from Zermatt, to Furi, to Trockener Steg and into Italy
0hr 40min		Zum See	
0hr 55min		Furi	
3hr 45min		Trockener Steg	
4hr 10min		Gandegghütte	

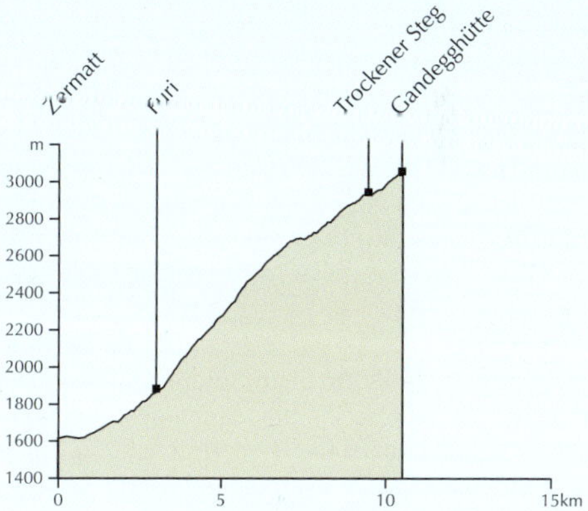

The traditional buildings and pastures of Zum See

Zermatt to Furi

55min, 3km, +265m -15m

From Zermatt's central square next to the church, head towards the Matterhorn up the main road signed for Trockener Steg and Gandegghütte. Just before the bridge which leads to the cable car station, bear right and continue along the quieter road. A kilometre from the start, at a path junction by a bench, continue straight on towards Zum See. The road soon gives away to a well-made track that rises smoothly between pastures, the Zmuttbach gorge to the left and the Matterhorn ahead. Once the path re-enters the trees you will reach a junction 25min from the start, where the route takes the left fork signed to Zum See.

Cross over the bridge and continue up the hill to another junction. Turn right to **Zum See** (1764m, **40min**, refreshments) and ascend into the tiny picturesque hamlet past the restaurants. Bear left through buildings towards a signpost and steps headed right, up the hill. The next signpost is reached at a T-junction above the steps with Furi signed left and Gandegghütte signed right. Taking the right-hand option will skip Furi and ascend via the mountain inn of Hermetje (refreshments). For the main route, turn left and up more steps. Continue up the well-made path until the road under the enormous cable car station is reached. Turn right and continue into **Furi** (1862m, **55min**, refreshments, accommodation, cable car).

Furi to Trockener Steg

2hr 50min, 6.5km, +1080m -15m

At the signpost next to Restaurant Furi, turn left signed towards Gandegghütte and immediately turn right up the hill. At the next junction with a small road, Gandegghütte is signed both to the left and straight on. Go straight on between two traditional outbuildings (the left route follows the vehicle access track and is best left for poor weather and snow only).

Steadily gaining ground above Zermatt, the Dom, Täschhorn and Rimpfischhorn in the distance

Further up the hill at the next junction, turn left continuing to climb through pastures and forest. Views open up to the left with early sight of the giants that will dominate the skyline today. After climbing steeply up through the trees, at the next junction the path which bypassed Furi rejoins the main route from the right, and the TMR continues straight on signed for Trockener Steg and Gandegghütte. The path soon leaves the trees and ascends the hillside with views ahead to the Breithorn, Castor, Pollux, and Liskamm, and behind towards the Matterhorn, with the Täschhorn, the Dom, and the Rimpfischhorn on the skyline.

Continue to ascend and traverse the hillside. The path will cross the Furggbach on a wooden bridge (2272m) and climb up to a junction with a track, where the route turns right. A few paces beyond, leave the track onto a footpath to the left, that rises above the track. The path ascends in zigzags with the Matterhorn dominating the view in one direction, and behind, increasing views of the peaks to the western side of the Zermatt valley, including the Weisshorn, the Ober Gabelhorn and the Zinalrothorn.

At the next signpost (2452m), go left signed to Gandegghütte. Now views to the Dent Blanche peek out above Schwarzsee station to the west. The path continues to wind its way upwards and round the grassy mountainside, with a series of extremely well-placed benches offering the opportunity for a picnic or taking in the views. Keep an eye out however; there can be mountain bikers descending this path at speed. At 2700m, the path enters rocky terrain as it traverses under the crag with Trockener Steg perched above.

After passing through the rocky area with the path going around boulders and over rock slabs (this can be difficult to navigate in poor visibility and snow), reach a junction with Trockener Steg visible on your right. If you continue straight on, the path leads direct to Gandegghütte. By turning right, you can go up to **Trockener Steg** (2929m, **3hr 45min**, cable car, refreshments) for snacks and to pick up some water, as you will need to pay for bottled water at the refuge. **Tip: the water in the restaurant bathroom at Trockener Steg is drinking water, available to patrons of the café (the tap water from the facilities by the shop on the ground floor is not drinking water).**

Trockener Steg to Gandegghütte **25min, 1km, +105m -5m**

While Trockener Steg and its surrounds are generally quite grim, even the grey of ski pistes, concrete, and hum of cable cars cannot distract from the majesty of the view around you, and the first look up to the Theodulgletscher. To continue for the final stretch to Gandegghütte with Trockener Steg behind you, keep to the left of the Matterhorn Test Centre and take the footpath directly ahead instead of the wider track which bears right.

The route is well marked with paint, cairns, and posts as it winds upward through boulders and moraine. The marigold yellow of Gandegghütte soon appears ahead, dwarfed by the Breithorn. When the path reaches a track, turn left towards the hut. Just before you arrive, the onward path to Theodulpass and the next stage is indicated to the right with the blue signpost (the Rif del Teodulo is about 1hr 30min away from this point, the other side of the Theodulgletscher). A few paces further, and you arrive at **Gandegghütte** (3028m, **4hr 10min**).

THE MATTERHORN

Arguably the most recognisable mountain in the world, the Matterhorn's unique silhouette – a natural pyramid of sheer rock faces and its tilted summit – is an icon of the Alps. People around the world flock to Zermatt to experience the sight, and there is nothing quite like seeing the joy and surprise on visitors' faces when they realise that yes, the reality of the mountain truly lives up to the hype.

While the great mountains of the Alps were conquered one by one during the golden age of alpinism in the mid-19th century, the Matterhorn seemed all but impregnable, and teams of mountaineers vied for the chance to be the first to meet the challenge. The first ascent was claimed by Englishman Edward Whymper and his team from Zermatt, but not without cost, when four of the seven climbers were lost during the descent. With success and disaster entwined, this event marks the end of that golden age. To date, an estimated 500-plus people have lost their lives on the mountain, making it one of the most lethal in the world.

Of the main faces of the Matterhorn pyramid, which broadly correspond with the compass points, the lowest is the east face, at 1000m, followed by the north (1200m, and one of the most dangerous north faces in the Alps), the south (1350m) and the west (1400m). From every angle, it stands singular and alone. Most ascents of the mountain go up the Hörnli ridge from the Hörnlihütte, between the east and north faces.

During the TMR, all but the west face will be visible, and hikers will be able to take in the different facets of the mountain, particularly on Stages 1 and 2. The iconic point will be visible again on many of the cols on the Italian side, and reappear once more at Hannigalp on Stage 9, as you turn south and into the Mattertal once again. It is an excellent lodestone to guide the final two days of the trek along the Europaweg, leading ever closer to Zermatt and the end of the Tour.

STAGE 2

Gandegghütte to Resy

Start	Gandegghütte (3028m)
Finish	Resy (2066m)
Walking time	7hr
Distance	20.5km
Ascent	680m
Descent	1640m
High point	Rifugio del Teodulo (3319m)
Variant	Alternative finish at St Jacques (1689m)

From Switzerland, the TMR enters Italy over the highest point on the Tour, after traversing the grey slopes of the Theodulgletscher with the Matterhorn and Breithorn standing watch. In case of poor conditions on the glacier or with the weather, the glacier crossing and Theodulpass can be wholly avoided by taking the cable car from Trockener Steg into Italy. If conditions are stormy, this may not run and you will face the question of rescheduling the trek or taking a combination of trains and buses around the massif.

Unfortunately, the first few kilometres in Italy are a grim sight; the terrain between the Theodulpass and the Colle Superior delle Cime Bianche is a monochrome stretch of grey and barren rock, under continuous work from machinery maintaining the ski area. The contrast once the Colle is passed is striking, with clear turquoise lakes and grassy, flower-strewn pastures; perhaps what the area around the Laghi delle Cime Bianche once looked like. The long descent towards Resy is continually beautiful with good paths the whole way, and the whole makes for an incredibly varied day.

CROSSING GLACIERS

Glaciers are inherently unstable and should not be underestimated. Before choosing this route option, please see the 'Glacier crossing' section in the Introduction for advice and identifying safe conditions.

Gandegghütte to Rif del Teodulo (Theodulhütte) **1hr 30min, 3.4km, +330m -40m**

On leaving Gandegghütte, go straight ahead and onto the blue signed route to the Theodulpass. There are very few paint markers as the route traverses rubble and

Facilities Stage 2			
0hr	⯅	Gandegghütte	
1hr 30min	⯅	Rifugio del Teodulo	
2hr 40min	🍴 🚡	Laghi delle Cime Bianche	
7hr	⯅	Resy	Rifugio Ferraro and Rifugio Guide di Frachey

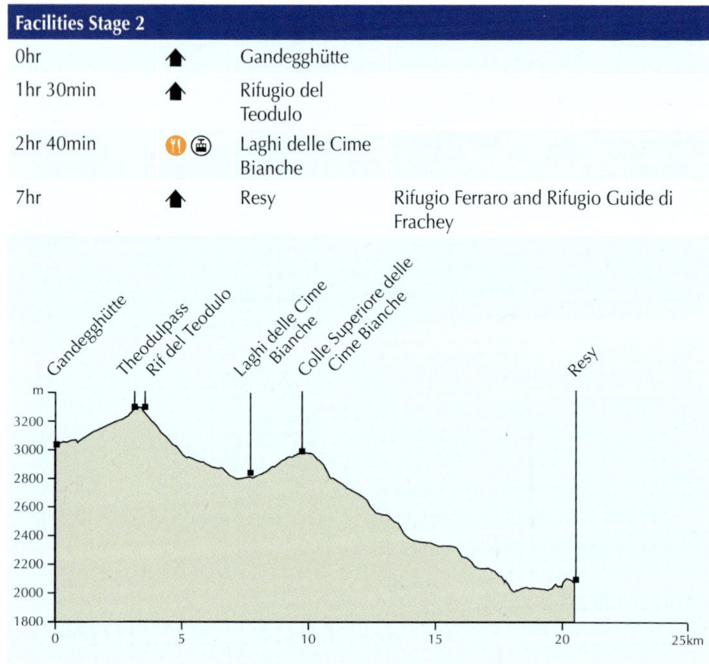

boulders, so keep an eye out for rock cairns, and red posts in the ground. You will be ascending to the right of a large bank of red rock until the rock and moraine falls away and the expanse of the Theodulgletscher lies ahead. The descent to the glacier is largely pathless; watch for cairns or marker posts, pick your own line or follow footsteps where others have gone before.

Once you have reached the glacier put on your crampons or spikes and traverse gently upwards across the **Theodulgletscher** until you reach the piste track towards the left side (west) of the glacier. Continue to ascend. Do not follow the piste all the way to Testa Grigia; when Rif del Teodulo comes into view, cut right and ascend the snow bank beneath the hut in zigzags. On reaching a track, take off your spikes, and walk the few paces up to the **Theodulpass** (3295m). To get to the continuing path into Italy, continue to the right, and for access to the rifugio, turn right again up a sharp ascent, to enjoy an Italian cappuccino at **Rif del Teodulo** (3319m, **1hr 30min**).

Hirli
2890m
2702m
Matterhorngletscher
Gornera
Riffelhorn
2927m
Matterhorn
4478m
SWITZERLAND
Trockener Steg
2929m
Gornergletscher
Furgggletscher
Gandegghütte
3028m
Furggen
3492m
Theodulgletscher
Unter Theodulegletcher
Schwärzegletscher
Theodulhorn
3472m
ITALY
Bontadini
3043m
Rif del Teodulo
3319m
Breithorngletscher
Klein Matterhorn
3883m
Breithorn
4160m
Gendarm
4106m
Torrente Barmaz
Theodulpass
3295m
il-Cervinia
Testa Grigia
3480m
Pollux
4092m
Lago Goillet
Laghi delle Cime Bianche
Laghi delle Cime Bianche
2808m
Gobba de Roin
3899m
Zwillingsgletscher
Ghiacciaio d'Aventina
Colle Superiore delle Cime Bianche
2982m
Gran Sometta
3166m
Gran Lago
Torrente di Tzere
Torrente d. Verra
La Roisettaz
3312m
Piano di Tzère
Monte Rosso
3034m
Torrente Curtod
Grand Tournalin
3879m
Colle di Bettaforca
2672m
N
Resy
2066m
Monte Bettaforca
Saint-Jacques
1689m
0
1
2
km
2971m
Passo del Rothorn
2689m
Torrente d' Nana
Becca di Nana
3010m
Torrente Evancon
Valle d'Ayas
Rothorn
3152m

The pisted track on the Theodulgletscher, looking down to Trockener Steg, with the Dent Blanche (left), Ober Gabelhorn (centre-left), Zinalrothorn (centre-right), and Weisshorn (right)

The **Theodulpass** is one of the ancient passes in the Alps, in use for centuries as a passage between the Swiss Valais and the Valle d'Aosta, particularly before the 1400s when the climate was warmer and the Theodul lost its glacier. Even when the glacier re-established itself, records of trade, travel and migration throughout the Middle Ages provide clear evidence of the importance of the route (though it remained secondary to the Great Saint Bernard Pass). Travel dropped off during the Little Ice Age, where the ice reached its peak around the year 1645. In the nineteenth century, the Theodul caught the attention of both mountaineers and tourists as a high but accessible route for touring and accessing the higher peaks.

Rif del Teodulo to Laghi delle Cime Bianche **1hr 10min, 4.3km, +20m -530m**

Descend on the access track with the Matterhorn directly ahead of you, with sporadic yellow arrows pointing the way. The Matterhorn looks quite different from its Italian side than the iconic Swiss view you have become used to. You will shortly reach **Bontadini** (3043m, restaurant is closed in summer) with its small chapel.

A few paces beyond the restaurant, leave the track and turn left down the path signed TMR. Watch carefully for this junction, it is easy to miss. Follow this path southwards, signage can be sporadic. The path joins a wider track next to a meltwater lake; continue straight along the track as it bends right and past another small lake, then bends left around a rise. Ignore the two tracks to the left and continue alongside the outflow stream before turning left, the track passing below and to the left of an abandoned cable car station. More TMR signs point you onwards, as the **Laghi delle Cime Bianche** come into view. Continue along the track by the lakefront towards the cable car station, and adjoining restaurant (2808m, **2hr 40min**).

ENGINEERING IN THE HIGH ALPS

When looking at the high peaks in the Alps; rocky pinnacles, 1000m-high cliffs and hulking glaciers, it seems impossible for people to build anything in such places. And yet, there are high mountain huts like the Gandegg throughout the region that have stood for over 150 years. Or further back, fortifications and roads that snake over high passes. The highest hut in the Alps is the Margherita Hut, on the summit of Monte Rosa's Signalkuppe (4554m), and the original building was opened in 1889 by Queen Margherita of Savoy. The hut was constructed in sections in the valley, and then transported by vast mule teams, and then teams of men for the final section, before being assembled on site. It remains the highest building in Europe, and is a testament to the incredible efforts of those members of the Italian Alpine Club in the late 19th century.

In many respects, the manner of building in the high Alps has not changed much in the intervening years; modern constructions will often build modular sections elsewhere, and transport them to the site – now by helicopter. The most recent challenge was the development of the Matterhorn Glacier Ride II cable car from Zermatt to Cervinia that became operational in summer 2023. This involved excavating and building a lift station into the rock of the Klein Matterhorn, before building the rest of the infrastructure, subject to all the wind and weather you'd expect at 3880m. Advances in construction meant that no intermediate cable car pylons were needed, and the whole system, including stations, is run off solar energy.

Laghi delle Cime Bianche to Colle Superiore delle Cime Bianche

40min, 1.9km, +180m -5m

From the cable car station drop down a few paces then bear left on the wide track which starts to climb. Waymarks are hard to find during this section, but continue along the track. When the track forks, take the lower option to the right, which, looking ahead, starts to zigzag up the hill. On a corner with a cairn with yellow arrows, you can see the pass straight ahead with a few cairns leading the way. After a large cairn, keep an eye out for the path leading right and away from

The idyllic Grand Lago and Gobba di Rollin above

the track. The path traverses and gently climbs up the hillside, with more regular waymarks. The final approach to the colle is largely flat.

On reaching a reservoir at **Colle Superiore delle Cime Bianche** (2982m, **3hr 20min**), which may or may not have water in it, the TMR skirts to the left-hand side. At the other side of the reservoir, cross under the chair lift lines and continue up the small rise. On reaching this, the view opens up towards the row of valleys and ridgelines on the Italian side of the TMR, with spectacular turquoise lakes (the Gran Lago and the Lac de la Pointe-de-Rollin) to the left under the dome of the Gobba de Rollin.

Colle Superiore delle Cime Bianche to Resy **3hr 40min, 10.9km, +150m -1065m**

The path soon drops down in tight zigzags to the outflow of the Gran Lago, where you cross the stream over the rocks. This makes for an excellent picnic spot. The descending path is idyllic; the route balances between steep drops and flat sections, crossing over grassy hillsides and alongside crystal clear streams.

Nearly 6km from the colle, reach a signpost with the main TMR signed left to Pian di Verraz and Resy. Route 6 (straight on) can otherwise take you to Saint-Jacques. A few minutes after the left turn, at a path junction next to a stream, keep right and start to descend into a stunning pretty hanging valley, the **Piano di Tzère**. The lush meadow is cloistered by pine trees, with a river cutting through the middle. A little paddling in the crystal-clear water may be irresistible!

After the open meadow, the path descends alongside the stream, using large stone blocks of stairs. When you come to a viewpoint with your first clear view of the (Ayas) valley, with Saint-Jacques and Champoluc, the path turns away from the river and follows the side of the mountain round to the left.

Now on a forest path, the route continues to traverse until it reaches a junction (**5hr 50min**), with Saint-Jacques signed right 40mins away. If you plan to finish the stage at Saint-Jacques, turn right on Routes 7 and 8 here. The TMR continues straight on (left). Soon the head of the valley comes into view, with the Breithorn to the left, Pollox centre, and Castor to the right. The view opens up substantially as you emerge from the trees into an expansive meadow with the mountains at the head. The onward route to Resy is across the bridge to the right, and there is further information about Monte Rosa and the special area of conservation on a sign just ahead.

After the bridge, the route descends a broad track. At a water fountain next to a signpost, leave the track left on a forest path signed TMR and Rifugio Ferraro (signed 20min). The path climbs fairly steeply up through the trees. The route is shaded and easy to follow, and in under 30mins you arrive at the charming Walser hamlet of **Resy** and its two rifugios overlooking the Valle d'Ayas (2066m, **7hr**).

THE VALLE D'AYAS

The first of the four Italian valleys on the TMR, the wide and forested Valle d'Ayas starts with the Breithorn, Castor and Pollux at its head and follows the Évançon downstream to meet the Aosta valley at Verrès. As the French name suggests, it has been a historic melting-pot of different cultures. The Romans conquered the valley from the Salassi people by 25BC, and the Theodulpass was in regular use as a strategically and commercially important passage to the Valais, with Roman coins discovered on the high reaches of the pass. For much of the valley's history since AD515, control and ownership of the land has been held by the Church (specifically, the Abbey of Saint-Maurice d'Agaune, and then the Bishop of Aosta, whose influence can be seen in the many significant and artistic churches in the valley), and the powerful Challant family, Viscounts of Aosta, who built a series of castles. A quieter influence, but one more relevant to Resy and Saint-Jacques for the TMR, were the Walser migrations into the valley which may have started as early as the 6th century, and certainly took place in the

12th century, which contributed to the Valais-style architecture (especially the *rascard* storage granaries – built of timber, and perched on small stilts above the ground), and the Germanic language (Saint-Jacques' full name is Saint-Jacques-des-Allemands).

Resy is perched above the valley on a sunny, south-facing slope, and offers two excellent choices for accommodation; the Rifugio Ferraro and the Rifugio Guide di Frachey, with far-reaching views from their terraces. Both can provide a packed lunch for the following day, otherwise, the nearest supplies will be in Champouloc, for which you will need to drop down to Saint-Jacques on the valley floor below Resy, and either walk 5km down the valley, or take the bus. Both Saint-Jacques and Champouloc have accommodation options if needed, and there are regular buses down to Verrès in the Aosta valley.

Rif Ferraro at Resy

STAGE 3

Resy to Alpe Gabiet

Start	Resy (2066m)
Finish	Alpe Gabiet (2350m)
Walking time	5hr 30min
Distance	14.7km
Ascent	1285m
Descent	1000m
High point	Passo del Rothorn (2689m)
Variant	Alternative route via Colle di Bettaforca (2675m); alternative finish at Oresteshütte (2600m)

From Resy, there is a choice of passes between the Valle d'Ayas and Valle del Lys; the a is more direct and has chairlift options, the Rothorn is a far better route. The TMR is now entering the heart of Walser territory in the upper Italian valleys, and you will find their influence everywhere; from architecture to the Germanic dialect.

Once past the Rothorn, there are plenty of options to stop for lunch and take in the immense view of Liskamm at the head of the valley. After dropping down to Stafal, there is a final climb at the end of the day up to the dispersed Alpe Gabiet, and Lago Gabiet (Gabietsee).

Resy to Passo del Rothorn **2hr 15min, 5.6km, +725m -100m**

A few paces beyond Rif Ferraro, you have a choice on which pass to take to the Gressoney valley (Valle del Lys). To carry on straight ahead will take you over the variant route Colle di Bettaforca, described as the variant below (which has chair-lift and cable car options both up and down). Or turn right on the main TMR route towards the Passo del Rothorn, signed 2hr 55min.

After five minutes, turn sharp left up the hill: do not continue on the route signed GSW. The path ascends on a small rise surrounded by pastures, with a river audible to the right. After 20min from Resy, reach a bridge crossing the river with a sign for TMR pointing straight ahead up the hill. On reaching a track turn left for a few paces, the TMR then continues to the right at the next track corner.

Two km and 40min from Resy, reach **La Mandria** (refreshments). The route continues past the restaurant, along and up the hill through beautiful pastures and pine. On reaching a track with the pyramid of the Testa Grigia ahead (a different

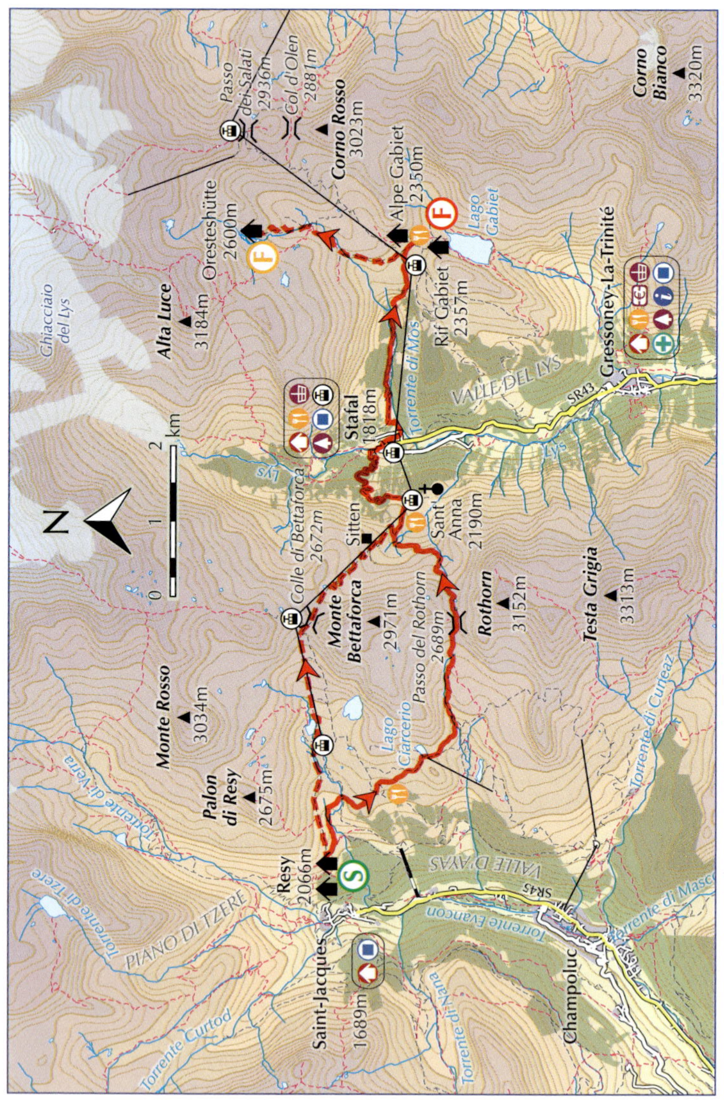
Passo dei Salati 2936m
Col d'Olen 2881m
Corno Rosso 3023m
Corno Bianco 3320m
Ghiacciaio del Lys
Oresteshütte 2600m
Alpe Gabiet 2350m
Lago Gabiet
Alta Luce 3184m
Rif Gabiet 2357m
Torrente di Mos
Gressoney-La-Trinité
VALLE DEL LYS
SR43
Lys
Stafal 1818m
0 1 2 km
N
Colle di Bettaforca 2672m
Sitten
Sant' Anna 2190m
Monte Bettaforca 2971m
Passo del Rothorn 2689m
Rothorn 3152m
Testa Grigia 3313m
Monte Rosso 3034m
Lago Ciarcerio
Torrente di Cuneaz
Palon di Resy 2675m
Torrente di Verra
Resy 2066m
VALLE D'AYAS
SR45
Torrente di Tzere
PIANO DI TZERE
Torrente Evançon
Torrente di Mascognaz
Saint-Jacques 1689m
Champoluc
Torrente di Nana
Torrente Curtod

peak to the Testa Grigia above the Theodul glacier), turn right. Be sure to look behind you to taking the view of the Breithorn, Castor, Pollux, as well as the route you descended yesterday.

At the top of the rise, reach Lago Ciarcerio (2376m) next to a winter-only chair lift. The TMR continues right and starts down the track. It will turn left shortly, signed towards Passo del Rothorn. The onward path rises and curves round the hillside, covered with an abundance of heather, bilberries, and a wide range of alpine flowers. The route is marked with cairns and yellow arrows, and you soon get a view up the minor valley towards the pass.

On crossing a stream you reach a signpost, pointing left towards the pass. The path criss-crosses the stream a few more times, around shrubs, rocks and boulders. It will soon start to climb more steeply, with the stream on the left, and yellow arrows pointing the way.

Approaching the pass, the Rothorn looms on the right, with some nameless peaks to the left before the summit of Monte Bettaforca on the far left. On the final approach to the pass, the grass and rocky hillside gives away to rocky rubble.

Facilities Stage 3

0hr		Resy	
40min		La Mandria	
3hr 15min		Sant'Anna	
3hr 50min		Stafal	
5hr 30min		Alpe Gabiet	Albergo del Ponte, Rif Gabiet (+10min)
(+50min)		Oresteshütte	

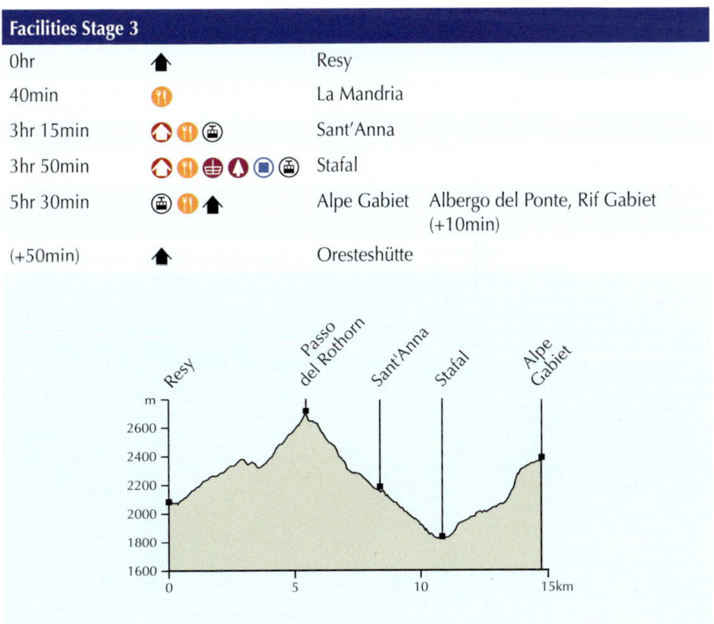

Nevertheless, the route is well marked with tall cairns and arrows as you cross several areas of boulders. The final climb of the **Passo del Rothorn** (2689m, **2hr 15min**) goes up a grassy bank until you reach the pass and the view beyond.

Passo del Rothorn to Sant'Anna

1hr, 2.7km, +5m -505m

The onward path drops down to the very picturesque Laghetti del Salero in tight zigzags. Passing the lakes, the route descends again hugging the left-hand side of the hill. Looking ahead you can see Alpe Gabiet on the other side of the Valle del Lys (Valle di Gressoney). As the route continues round, more views open up towards the north-east, including Monte Rosa and Liskamm.

As Sant'Anna and the cable car stations come into view, the path descends more steeply, with deep steps and a drop to the right. The path continues down, crossing meadows filled with butterflies and flowers, until it reaches a track. Left will take you to Hotel-Restoro Sitten (2304m, refreshments, accommodation) in a few minutes, but right is the onward route to **Sant'Anna** (2190m, **3hr 15min**, refreshments, cable car to Stafal), named for the chapel overlooking the valley.

> The tiny white chapel at **Sant'Anna** (Cappella di Sant'Anna), a few minutes from the TMR, was built in 1726 and has dramatic views to the surrounding cols, Liskamm, and down the Gressoney valley. A plaque commemorates the visit in 2001 of Pope John Paul II.

Sant'Anna to Stafal

35min, 2.5km, -370m

At a track junction alongside the Restaurant Jutz, the TMR continues left down the track to Stafal. On a clear day, the view will be dominated by Liskamm. The route

Stafal in the Lys valley, looking towards Liskamm

descends on a broad but stony track and zigzags down. On reaching a car park, walk through and turn right at the road, and continue down to the bridge into the busy hamlet of **Stafal** (Staffal on some maps) (1818m, **3hr 50min**, refreshments, accommodation, cable car, bus, outdoor shop, groceries). The onward TMR route is on the left bank of the Lys river.

Stafal to Alpe Gabiet **1hr 40min, 3.9km, +555 -25m**

After the Ambarddanspitz sport shop, food shop (alimentari), and Hotel Nordend complex, turn left signed 1hr 40 to Alpe Gabiet on the TMR. The grassy path passes between Alpine homes, and heads towards a small chapel which dates from 1643. At a road, turn left signed TMR and leave it again a few paces later on a track, straight ahead. The route to Alpe Gabiet has a number of watchful guardians; where tree stumps have been carved with faces.

The route becomes an uncompromising pull uphill, the track does not last long, but the path onwards is indicated left signed 7A and 7B. This is even steeper and zigzags up a field to meet a track next to a wooden barrier. Turn right, signed 7A and TMR. At the next bend of the track follow it round, and keep an eye out for a yellow arrow indicating the onward path to the right a few paces after the bend. This footpath winds upwards through pretty forest and rock-strewn meadow, staying above the track and Endrebach river (Torrente di Mos).

Just over 2km from Stafal, the path drops down to the track and crosses the river still signed 7A. After undulating for a few more minutes, the path begins to steepen, and will get steeper the further up you go. Eventually, the route levels out and it is just a few minutes further into **Alpe Gabiet** (2350m, **5hr 30min**, cable car, refreshments, accommodation). This is a dispersed collection of buildings across a wide area, with several refreshment options – including one overlooking Lago Gabiet – and two accommodation options: Albergo del Ponte and **Rif Gabiet** (2357m, **+10mins from Alpe Gabiet**).

Variant: Resy to Sant'Anna via the Colle di Bettaforca **3hr, 6.5km, +600m -500m**

The Bettaforca col gives a quicker and easier route into the Lys valley than the Passo del Rothorn, and is also served by chairlifts on either side. The crossing is mainly on tracks, and is a marked alternative of the TMR. The variant doesn't have the wildness of the Passo del Rothorn, and is of most value in poor conditions where the trekker is still looking to make progress along the route.

Turn left out of the refuge and take the wide track rather than the signed Rothorn route. After 40min approach a reservoir and keep to the right of it, keeping the lift station on your right. Find a rather poorly marked turn and head steeply uphill (**45min**, if you reach the stream above the reservoir backtrack to the turn).

The reservoir at Alpe Forca superiore on the ascent of the Colle di Bettaforca variant

Climb alongside the chairlift to the col at 2675m (**1hr 45min**). The chairlift stations are above to the left. The onwards route to Sant'Anna continues on the track on the other side of the pass. After 40min come to **Hotel-Ristoro Sitten** (2304m, refreshments, accommodation). From the hotel, the track continues to descend beneath the chairlift, past the junction where the Passo del Rothorn path rejoins on the right, to reach the **Sant'Anna** restaurant (Jutz), and the top of the Stafal cable car (**3hr**). The Sant'Anna chapel is 5min to the right.

Variant: to Oresteshütte **50min, 3km, +200m**

The **Oresteshütte** (2600m) is another 50min, 3km and 200m of ascent beyond Alpe Gabiet. From Gabiet, take a track left, signed towards the hut on route 6B. Despite this added distance, it is in a beautifully wild spot, under Piramide Vincent. The refuge was built in 2006 to an excellent standard and offers accommodation and fully vegan cuisine. For the onward connection to Col d'Olen for Stage 4, instead of returning back to Alpe Gabiet, you can turn left on the descent from Orestes, on a track just after the small reservoir, which rejoins the TMR on the ascent to the pass.

THE GRESSONEY (LYS) VALLEY

The head of the Lys valley is blocked with the immense wall of Liskamm and Piramide Vincent, some 2600m above Stafal, the highest village on the valley floor. The valley is far longer than neighbouring Valle d'Ayas, and winds down nearly 40km following the Lys river to Pont-Saint-Martin in the Valle d'Aosta. The valley is naturally stepped (like a series of enormous hanging valleys). Nowadays, those natural steps make the Lys valley an excellent natural hydro-electric system, starting with Lago Gabiet. Historically, the stepped geography made the upper reaches difficult to get to from the south, allowing the Walser migrants to settle and travel over passes between the upper Italian valleys, and for their cultural influence to be relatively undisturbed. Unlike the Valle d'Ayas to the west, there is no direct passage between the Lys valley over to the Valais, and without that strategic significance there would have been less trade and fewer visitors to the valley.

Consider the names encountered on the stage: Rothorn, Stafal, the Schwoarzehòre and Seehòre peaks about Gabiet, the two-language road signs; the Walser influence on the language and culture in the Gressoney valley is impossible to ignore, with Walser German (the *titsch* dialect) still occasionally spoken, and cultural traditions still a part of Gressoney life.

While there are more facilities in this stage than previous days – from multiple restaurants to the small Alimentaria shop in Stafal – for a wider range of options, you will need to walk downstream (or take a bus) from Stafal to Gressoney-La-Trinité which also has a small Walser museum, bank, tourist information centre, food shop, pharmacy, and far more accommodation options. Beyond Gressoney-La-Trinité, the next stop at Gressoney-St-Jean is a larger town, with a yet wider range of facilities.

Sant'Anna chapel overlooks the Gressoney valley

STAGE 4

Alpe Gabiet to Rifugio Pastore

Start	Alpe Gabiet (2350m)
Finish	Rifugio Pastore (1575m)
Walking time	7hr
Distance	18.3km
Ascent	990m
Descent	1765m
High point	Col d'Olen (2881m)
Variant	Options beyond Alagna to Rif Pastore

This stage aims to escape the world of ski lifts and pistes as soon as possible, through a direct climb up to the Col d'Olen (that said, it is possible to take a cable car all the way to Alagna from Alpe Gabiet if you choose). Once over the Col, the land opens up, gnarled ridges extending away in a stacked horizon. It will feel like a long way down to the town of Alagna (and it is), but there is plenty to delight: from ibex skipping over the rocks, to the Passo Foric's airy climb and the long descent through the lush green down to the extraordinarily picturesque alpine hamlets of Otro. The final push up the valley to the Rif Pastore may test already tired feet, but the rifugio is a charming and well deserved finish.

Alpe Gabiet to Col d'Olen — **1hr 40min, 3.5km, +530m -10m**

From the junction at Alpe Gabiet just down from the Albergo del Ponte, follow the TMR as it ascends an often steep and unrelenting track. 30mins from Alpe Gabiet, the link track to Oresteshütte joins from the left. After about an hour of climbing, at 2800m, where the track meets the line of the gondola lift, take a sharp right by a prominent cairn and continue to follow another track across a ski piste, before a path appears right to take you to the **Col d'Olen** (2881m, **1hr 40min**). Waymarks on this final stretch can be sporadic, extra care should be taken in poor visibility.

Col d'Olen to Passo Foric — **1hr 20min, 3.4km, +50m -500m**

The path from Col d'Olen traverses round to a viewpoint and the abandoned Rif Citta' di Vigevano (closed). Views are extensive and particularly dominated by the snowy Piramide Vincent to the north. Descend some stone steps and look for the red and white paint marker where our path doubles back to the right.

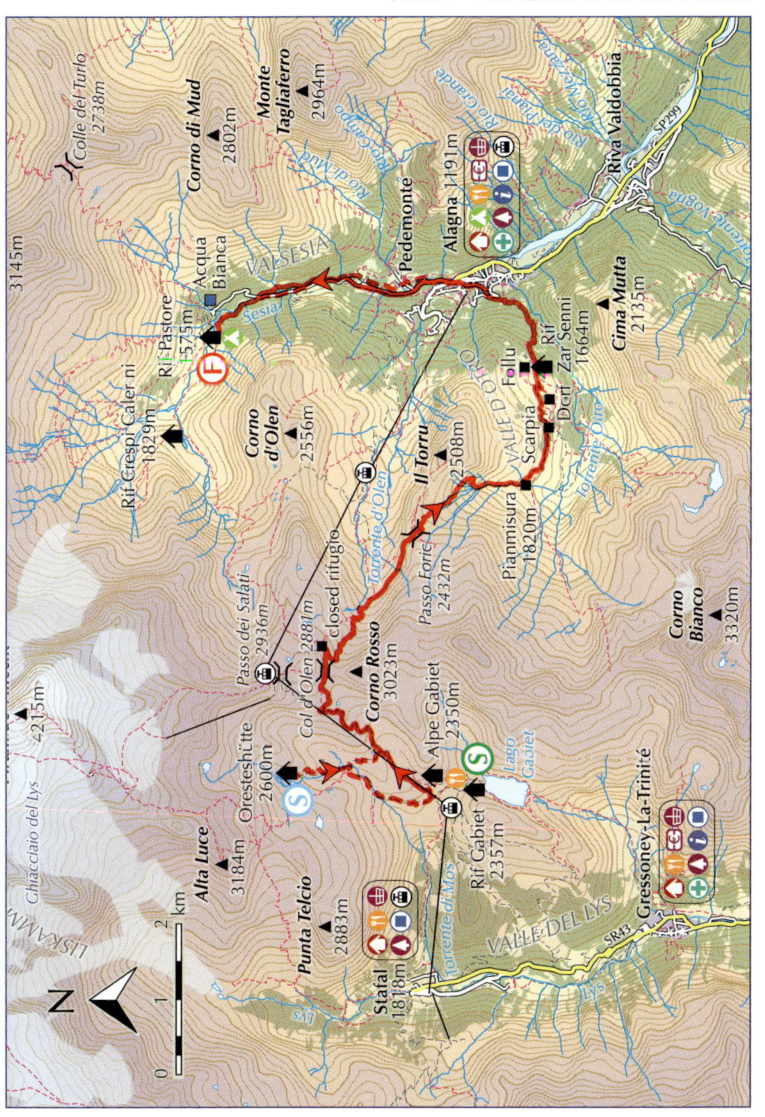
Colle del Turlo
2738m
Corno di Mud
2802m
Monte Tagliaferro
2964m
Rio Campo
Rio di Mud
Rio Grande
Rio del Pianal
Rio Mezzana
Riva Valdobbia
SP299
Torrente Vogna
Alagna 1191m
Pedemonte
VALSESIA
Sesia
Acqua Bianca
Rif Pastore
1575m
3145m
1829m
Corno d'Olen
2556m
Il Torru
2508m
Follu
Rif Zar Senni
1664m
Dorf
Scarpia
Cima Mutta
2135m
Torrente Otro
Pianmisura
1820m
Torrente d'Olen
Passo Foric
2432m
closed rifugio
Passo dei Salati
2936m
Col d'Olen 2881m
Corno Rosso
3023m
Alpe Gabiet
2350m
Lago Gabiet
Corno Bianco
3320m
Gressoney-La-Trinité
4215m
Oresteshütte
2600m
Alta Luce
3184m
Ghiacciaio del Lys
LISKAMM
Rif Gabiet
2357m
Torrente di Mos
Punta Telcio
2883m
Stafal
1818m
VALLE DEL LYS
SR43
Lys
N
0
1
2
km

Facilities Stage 4		
0hr		Alpe Gabiet
4hr 30min		Rif Zar Senni
5hr 30min		Alagna
7hr		Rif Pastore

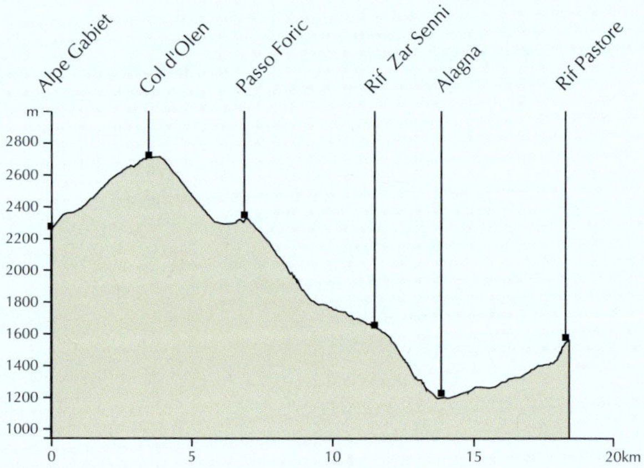

Alpe Gabiet
Col d'Olen
Passo Foric
Rif Zar Senni
Alagna
Rif Pastore

m
2800
2600
2400
2200
2000
1800
1600
1400
1200
1000

0
5
10
15
20km

The final path to the Col d'Olen

The path descends in zigzags down the side of the hill, accompanied by red and white paint splashes marked by the number 205. This can be a popular hillside for ibex herds, and look on the right for the Sasso del Diavolo (see below). About an hour from the Col d'Olen, reach a signpost and a painted sign on a rock with Passo Foric indicated to the right. You can see the route ahead, traversing the steep and grassy hill towards the stunning ridge line. The path up to the col has spectacular views to the left, and while there are a couple of points where fixed cables provide protection, it is only a short climb until the crest of the ridge at **Passo Foric** (2432m, **3hr**) is reached.

The **Sasso del Diavolo** (Devil's Stone) is a large boulder with a blackened crack, seen on the descent of the Col d'Olen. Local legend has it that the devil was so furious by the building of Gressoney's church that he found the biggest boulder he could on the Col d'Olen, intending to fling it down the mountain and crush the building work. An angel ordered him to stop, and in a fit of temper, the devil punched the boulder and it fell away towards Alagna, saving Gressoney's church.

Passo Foric to Rif Zar Senni

1hr 30min, 4.6km, +10m -775m

From the top of Passo Foric, the TMR, also labelled as path 3b, descends a beautiful grassy hillside accompanied by babbling streams and the sound of cow bells. The path can be steep and narrow in places, but wayfinding should not cause issues. Once the hamlet of **Alpe Pianmisura Piccola** (1820m, **4hr,** no facilities) is reached, the path broadens into a grassy track that bears left and gently descends the hill past a sequence of Alpe hamlets: Scarpia, Dorf, and culminating with Follu and the picture-perfect **Rif Zar Senni** (1664m, **4hr 30min,** refreshments, refuge).

VALLE D`OTRO AND WALSER ARCHITECTURE

The Valle d'Otro, a subsidiary valley to Alagna's Valsesia contains some of the best examples of preserved Walser buildings across its Alpe hamlets of Follu, Scarpia, Weng, Fellerech and Dorf. While a popular spot for visitors hiking from Alagna, these hamlets are still in use as farms and pastures; broadly unchanged since their establishment in the 14th century, when Walser migrants travelled to Valle d'Otro eastwards from Gressoney.

The TMR passes a range of classic Walser architecture in the Valle d'Otro, from animal barns and granaries to chapels and homes. Built from timber and stone, with a broad overhanding roof protecting slatted

The path to Passo Foric clambers up the craggy ridge

galleries, and some buildings half-buried in the hillside with grassy roofs, the fact that these buildings stand today is testament to the resilience of their designs against the Alpine climate, and the quality of their construction.

Rif Zar Senni to Alagna

1hr, 2.6km, +5m -470m

From the rifugio follow the track down as it descends in zigzags through leafy woodland. At a fountain at a junction turn left. TMR waypoints from here to the end of the stage are very scarce and the track is often chaotically paved with rocks and webbed with tree roots. At a four-way junction with a path left and right, and one heading further downhill, turn left past a shrine and continue to Alagna. At a lane, cross over and follow the path. Continue straight ahead through houses, crossing over a footbridge, dropping into central **Alagna** where the well-made stone path leads directly to the slate-roofed church (1191m, **5hr 30min**).

Note that Alagna is the last place to pick up supplies before Macugnaga, so remember to stock up. If staying at Rif Pastore, then a packed lunch for the following day can be arranged.

ALAGNA AND VALSESIA

Valsesia is the longest of the Italian valleys on the TMR, and from the Monte Rosa peaks of Signalkuppe (or Punta Gnifetti, 4554m), Parrotspitze (Punta Parrot, 4434m), and Piramide Vincent (4215m) at its head, it winds 50km south and east towards the Italian lakes and Po valley.

Before the arrival of the Walser, Valsesia belonged to the monasteries of San Nazzaro of Biandrate, San Pietro in Casteletto and to the Bishop of Novara. In the Medieval era, these were kept as high Alpine pastures, with few settlements (understandable since land at lower elevations and further south was far easier to live on). There are records from the 13th and 14th centuries that some of the Walser migration and settlement of Alagna and the upper Valsesia was instigated by the work of the monasteries, by transferring rights over grazing pastures to Walser peoples from Macugnaga (and, to a lesser extent, Gressoney). With established settlements taking root in the upper Italian valleys, so too could trans-Alpine trade over the high passes between the valleys, which in turn benefited the feudal lords and monasteries. While transhumance farming dominated, there are also several manganese mines in the valley, which were used for glass making and metal working.

Alagna played a key role in the early days of Italian mountaineering; the Guides Association was founded in 1872 and is the second oldest in Italy. Alagna also was, and remains, a key base for climbers approaching Monte Rosa and the Margherita Hut, and several first ascents of Monte Rosa peaks started in Alagna, including the very early 1801 ascent of Punta Giordani (4046m, next to Piramide Vincent) by Alagna resident Pietro Giordani, all the way to the most recent (and challenging) new route on the south-east face of Signalkuppe by Hervè Barmasse and his father in 2011.

Alagna has an excellent museum that explores more of the history and way of life of the Walser people. The town also has a good range of facilities, including a range of accommodation options, food and outdoor gear shops, pharmacy, bank, and tourist information centre.

There is a local shuttle bus service that can skip the road walking along the valley between Alagna and the Acqua Biancha waterfalls, so hikers can reach the charming Alpe buildings of Rif Pastore and its incredible views of Monte Rosa. Or alternatively, if staying in Alagna, it can cut a very long day over the Turlo to Macugnaga into just a long one. Information and timetables available at www.alagna.it/en/shuttle-service.

Monte Rosa at the head of Valsesia from Rif Pastore: Piramide Vincent (left), Parrotspitze (centre), Signalkuppe (right)

Alagna to Rif Pastore

1h 30min, 4.2km, +395m -10m

To leave Alagna, follow the road out of the town until you reach a children's playground and café (refreshments). Here you have a choice: the official route follows the road up the hill; a more pleasant variant takes the bridge on the right to Pedemonte and follows the other side of the river.

The road option has had diversions in the past due to rockfalls. If the route is clear, follow the road for just over 2km until the Sant'Antonio chapel on the left. After the chapel, the route to Rif Pastore is indicated left on route 6, climbing steeply to **Rifugio Pastore** (1575m, **7hr**, refuge, camping).

The route on the left bank (east) of the river can be joined at Pedemonte, or further along the road after the large car park at Merletti. If this option is taken, the road can be reached again by several bridges along the way.

If you are staying at Rif Pastore, cross the bridge at Sant'Antonio chapel (1391m) and turn right, climbing the final – gruelling at the end of a long stage – 175m to the refuge, with Monte Rosa's Signalkuppe presiding. If you are continuing on to the Colle del Turlo for Stage 5, it is recommended to continue on the right side of the river on route 7 to meet the path from Rif Pastore.

STAGE 5

Rifugio Pastore to Macugnaga

Start	Rifugio Pastore (1575m)
Finish	Macugnaga (1315m)
Walking time	7hr 30min
Distance	22km
Ascent	1245m
Descent	1505m
High point	Colle del Turlo (2738m)

Today's trek over the Colle del Turlo has to be one of the highlights of the TMR, if for nothing else but the appreciation of a remarkable feat of engineering. The route over the Turlo has been crafted by hand (specifically, a regiment of Alpini in the 1930s) in a drawn out ribbon of paved rock. Beyond the mountain craftsmanship, the Monte Rosa has never been so close, and its towering presence dominates throughout the day, from sunrise pink hues at Pastore, to the friendly town of Macugnaga – which is justifiably proud of its position at the foot of the soaring east face. It's a long day too, the 15km of downhill likely to test already tired legs, and even the novelty of the wriggling path may wear off after yet another zigzag.

Rif Pastore to Colle del Turlo

3hr, 7.2km, +1175m -10m

Leaving Rif Pastore, walk straight ahead towards Monte Rosa before bearing right to cross over the Sesia river on a covered bridge – this can be slippery when wet. The climb up to the pass begins here, with a couple of path junctions with waymarks painted on rocks. The path is a fantastic gradient for setting a good uphill pace. After about an hour, keep right over a stream also signed on a rock to the Turlo.

The path continues to be beautifully constructed and never goes beyond 15% of gradient, and there are no offshoots or other paths to contend with. Three hours from Pastore, you will reach the **Colle del Turlo** (2738m, **3hr**), a relief marker carved into the top commemorating the work of the fourth Alpini Regiment.

THE TURLO

In the Walser dialect, Turlo means 'little door', a sweet diminutive name for such a monumental pass. The Turlo has been in use for centuries, and it only takes looking a map (at quite a small scale), for the significance of the route to become clear: the Valsesia snakes east and south for over 50km to link into the Po valley and east to the Italian lakes. The Valle Anzasca on the other hand, with Macugnaga at its head, heads east for 30km to the Valle d'Ossola. Going the long way means a trip of 140km compared to the 25km from Alagna to Macugnaga over the Turlo. As such, the Turlo was a pivotal link for trade and Walser migrations through the Middle Ages – a fact recognised by a plaque on the pass commemorating a 1970s meeting of Walser peoples from surrounding settlements in Italy and Switzerland.

The route may have been well developed as a mule track already, but was built upon and transformed in the 1930s by the fourth Alpini Regiment (see the faded stone carving on the pass), who are responsible for much of the constructed route that exists today. The goal was to create a track with sufficient width and gradient for transporting small artillery.

Walking the Turlo pass is a wholly unique experience. The work of the Alpini has largely stood the test of 100 years of erosion and weather and now offers a long but consistent route with a hydra's worth of snaking zigzags. The construction is extraordinary and mainly brings to mind a Roman road. Far from cable cars or roads, this is a quiet and wild route, where ibex roam the high pastures and you can often find snow at the top well into the summer.

Ibex roam in the higher reaches of the Turlo

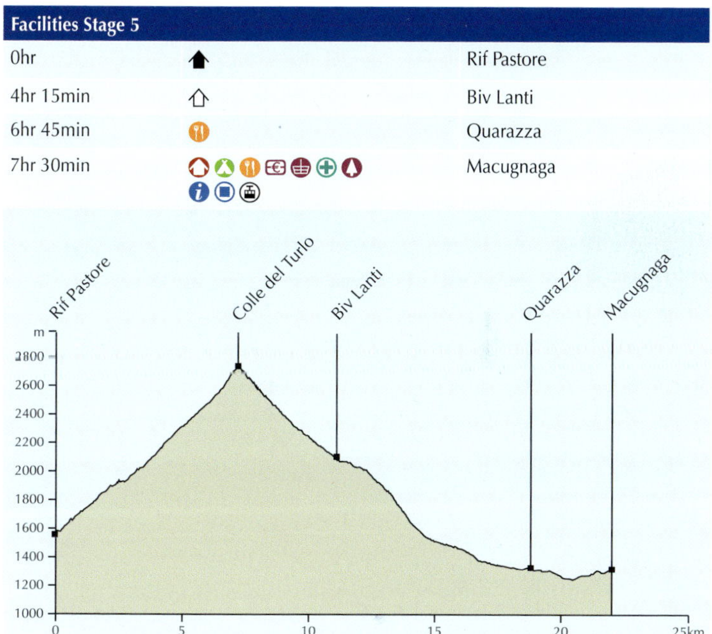

Facilities Stage 5		
0hr		Rif Pastore
4hr 15min		Biv Lanti
6hr 45min		Quarazza
7hr 30min		Macugnaga

Colle del Turlo to Quarazza

3hr 45min, 11.6km, -1415m

Descending from the pass, the soldiers of the Alpini regiment had clearly hit their stride, as the route down is in fantastic condition bearing many of the hallmarks of a Roman road. After approximately **1hr 15min** reach the **Bivacco Lanti** (2125m, unmanned bivouac/refuge), which has a new building with beds for nine, blankets included.

At 20min after the Bivacco, the route reaches the cluster of buildings at Alpe Schena at 2005m (or 2037m depending on which map you consult). A signpost indicates Macugnaga in two hours. At this point, the path again turns into a ribbon of switchbacks. As the land grows more vegetated, roots and the occasional stream have damaged the previously smoothly paved path, and it becomes quite disrupted and overgrown.

Alpe la Piana is reached at 1604m, roughly 5hr 30min from the start, as the route closes in on the Torrente Quarazza. In another half an hour, as the path shadows the river, you reach and cross a wooden footbridge. Keep an eye out on

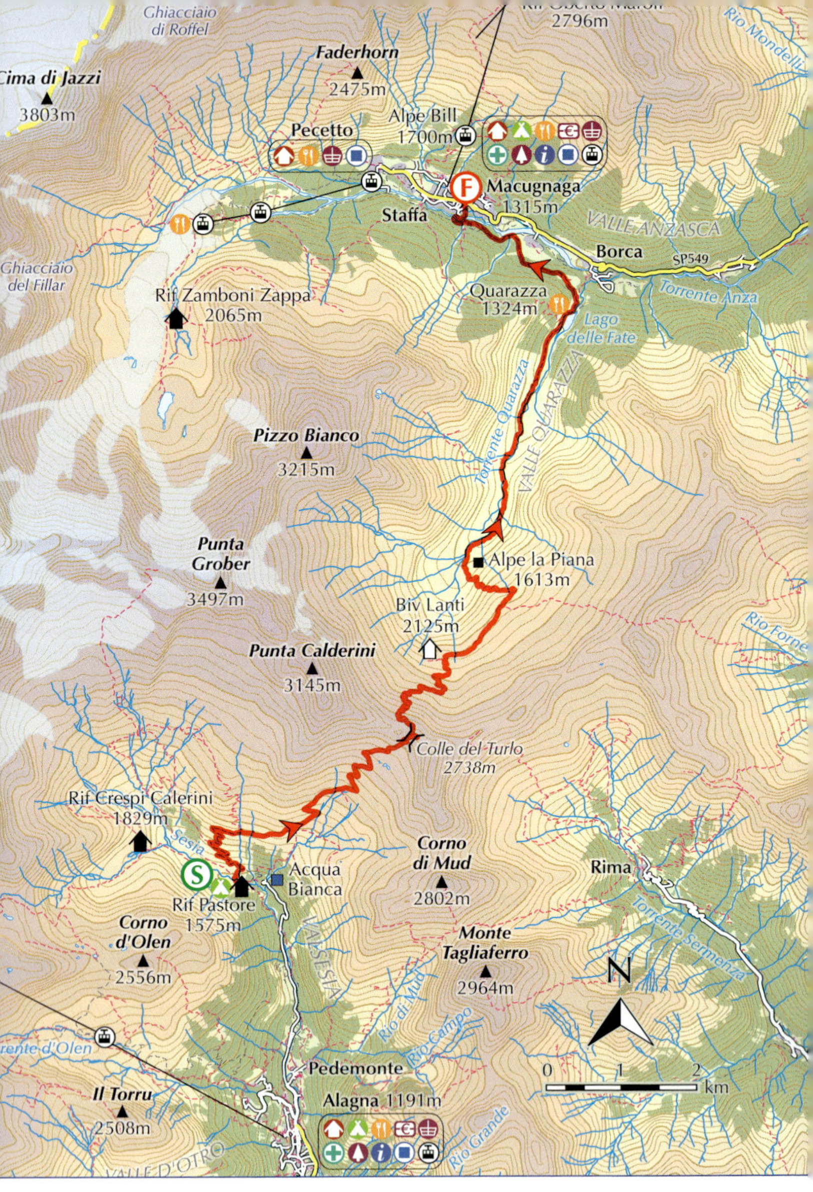

Ghiacciaio di Roffel
2796m
Rio Mondelli
Faderhorn
2475m
Cima di Jazzi
3803m
Pecetto
Alpe Bill
1700m
Macugnaga
1315m
Staffa
VALLE ANZASCA
Borca
SP549
Ghiacciaio del Fillar
Quarazza
1324m
Torrente Anza
Lago delle Fate
Rif Zamboni Zappa
2065m
Torrente Quarazza
VALLE QUARAZZA
Pizzo Bianco
3215m
Punta Grober
3497m
Alpe la Piana
1613m
Biv Lanti
2125m
Rio Forne
Punta Calderini
3145m
Colle del Turlo
2738m
Rif Crespi Calerini
1829m
Sesia
Corno di Mud
2802m
Rima
Acqua Bianca
Rif Pastore
1575m
Corno d'Olen
2556m
VALSESIA
Monte Tagliaferro
2964m
Torrente Sermenza
N
Rio di Mud
Rio Campo
rente d'Olen
Pedemonte
0
1
2
km
Il Torru
2508m
Alagna 1191m
Rio Grande
VALLE D'OTRO

The path on either side of the Colle del Turlo is incredibly consistent and well made

your right as the river tosses and foams down turquoise pools on smooth white rock. Pass an old mining location at Crocette, at 1360m, with interpretation boards discussing the previous industry. The track continues alongside the picture-perfect **Lago delle Fate** to reach the popular restaurants at **Quarazza** (1324m, **6hr 45min**, refreshments).

> **Valle Quarazza** may be a quiet and largely empty hanging valley now, but in the past miners struck gold and the area was most active from the 18th to the 20th century. In its most productive years in the 1940s, 400–580kg of gold ore was extracted from the main mine, Guia, per year. This mine is now a museum accessible from Macugnaga and is open for visitors.

Quarazza to Macugnaga — **45min, 3.2km, +70 -80m**

Shortly following the second bar at Quarazza, reach a junction where a path splits off right from the track. Both are signed to Macugnaga: continue on the track to the left.

The wide track may be a welcome change after walking on hard rock all day. Continue on towards Macugnaga at every junction as the track reaches the Torrente Anza, then pulls gently uphill, before crossing over a footbridge and doubling back on the other side. From here it is only a short, sharp kick to the centre of **Macugnaga** (1315m, **7hr 30min**).

If you plan to skip the climb up to Monte Moro and take the cable car to stay at Rif Oberto Maroli, be aware that the last cable car is at 16.15.

MACUGNAGA AND VALLE ANZASCA

Of all the Italian valleys on the TMR, each is headed by 4000m mountains in the Monte Rosa massif. Saving the best for the final valley, Macugnaga in the Valle Anzasca lies at the foot of the full east face of Monte Rosa; at 2400m (3300m between Macugnaga and the summit), this is the largest mountain wall in the Alps, a view of Himalayan proportions of which Macugnaga is rightly proud.

Macugnaga is another example of a Walser settlement, and with the many larch timber buildings still making up the villages, it's a very well preserved one. The main migrations coming through the Saastal over the Monte Moro pass happened in the 13th and 14th centuries. And from Macugnaga, people were then able to climb over the Turlo to settle Alagna. Macugnaga's old church (*Chiesa Vecchia*) was first built in the 13th century, and partially rebuilt in the 1600s. A 700-year-old linden tree stands beside it, and the cemetery commemorates several notable mountaineers and artists.

Macugnaga is a charming little town (or rather, a collection of smaller villages, including Staffa, Pecetto and Borca), with a full range of facilities, shops and accommodation options as well as a self-service laundry and museums on the Walser, and on mountains and smuggling. It's worth considering as an option to start the trail, or for a rest day to travel up to the Belvedere (walk or chair lift) and get close to the enormous east face of Monte Rosa. If you visit in the first week of July, you may catch the San Bernado Fair (*Fiera di San Bernado*). Links down the Valle Anzasca are by bus through to Domodossola; with both train and bus options north to Brig in Switzerland, and south to Milan and the Italian lakes.

STAGE 6

Macugnaga to Monte Moro (Rifugio Oberto Maroli)

Start	Macugnaga (1315m)
Finish	Rifugio Oberto Maroli (2796m)
Walking time	4hr
Distance	7.6km
Ascent	1490m
Descent	10m
High point	Rifugio Oberto Maroli (2796m)

A relatively short day, and a very simple mission – to climb the Passo Monte Moro. In clear weather this climb is accompanied by staggering views of Monte Rosa, from the start at Macugnaga all the way up. But the mountain is prone to hiding in cloud, so it's likely that the view will not last. While only 7.5km to the top, the 1500m climb should not be underestimated: this can be a stern ascent, though not technically difficult. A stay at Rif Oberto Maroli offers a great experience with (weather depending) peerless views across to the Monte Rosa massif. The climb, however, is not compulsory, and is covered entirely by a cable car from Macugnaga – see the note below for planning the next couple of days.

OPTIONS FROM MACUGNAGA TO SAAS-FEE

The ascent from Macugnaga to the Rif Oberto Maroli/Passo Monte Moro can either be completed as a short 4hr stage on its own, or combined with the onwards route to Saas-Fee or the Britanniahütte. If the latter, it is recommended that you take the cable car from Macugnaga either straight after Stage 5 for a night at Rif Oberto Maroli, or first thing in the morning (check times beforehand at https://macugnaga-monterosa.com, the first is usually at 08.30, with the last lift to Monte Moro at 16.15).

Walking the whole route from Macugnaga to Saas-Fee or the Britanniahütte would involve over 9hr of walking time and should only be attempted by very strong trekkers, however there is an option for a bus on the low-level route from Mattmark to Saas-Almagell and Saas-Fee.

Note, if you plan on the high-level route via Britanniahütte, Macugnaga is the last place to pick up supplies before Saas-Fee, so stock up with the food you will need on the trail.

Macugnaga to Alpe Bill

1hr 5min, 2.6km, +390m -5m

From the central square in Macugnaga next to the tourist information office, take the small road (signed *Chiesa Vecchia*) immediately to the left of the tourist office next to the bridge. Go past the old church (a far smaller and more picturesque building than the fortress in the centre of town), and continue along the lane until you reach the Tambach stream. Do not cross the bridge; the track up to Passo Monte Moro is signed to the right in 4hr 15min. A hundred metres later, take the path marked to the right, which becomes a familiar-looking paved mule track.

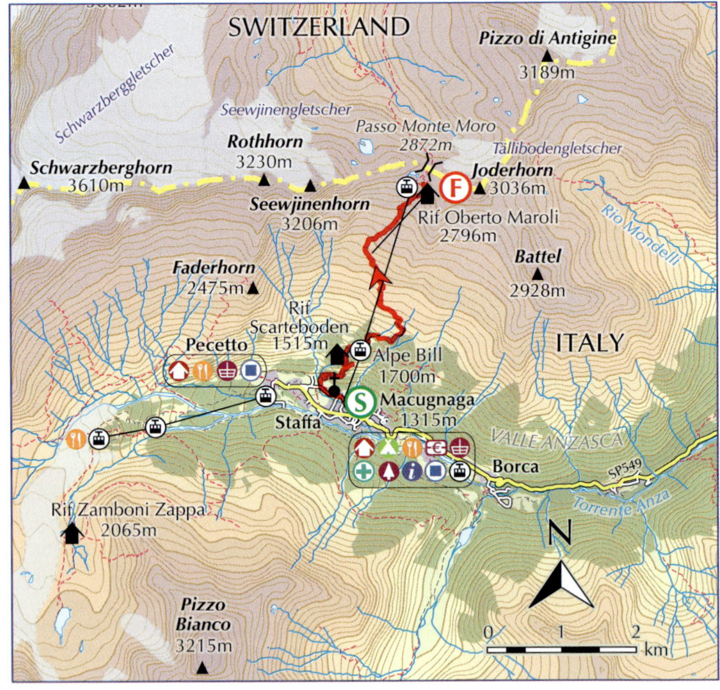

Rif Scarteboden is 30mins above Macugnaga, with views to Monte Rosa

Facilities Stage 6

0hr	Macugnaga
30min	Rif Scarteboden
1hr 5min	Alpe Bill
4hr	Rif Oberto Maroli
(+5min)	*Monte Moro cable car*

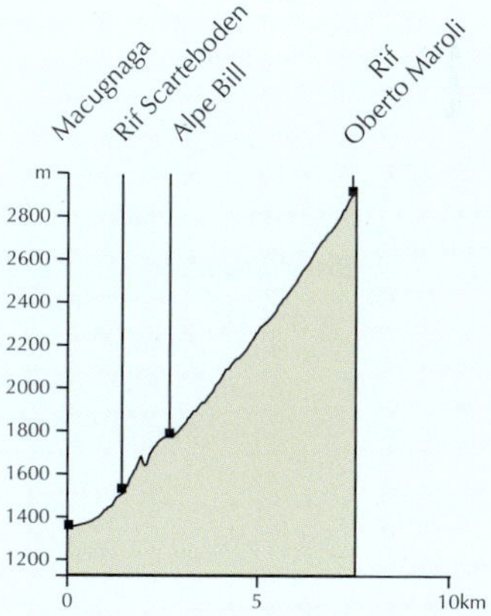

Macugnaga
Rif Scarteboden
Alpe Bill
Rif Oberto Maroli

m
2800
2600
2400
2200
2000
1800
1600
1400
1200
0
5
10km

MONTE ROSA'S EAST FACE

The 'Himalayan Wall' of the east face of Monte Rosa above Macugnaga is the grandest mountain wall in the Alps. In scale, it stretches 3km wide, and around 2500m tall from its base at the Ghiacciaio del Belvedere (the glacier itself is around 700m above Macugnaga). It would be tempting, when seeing the dawn light blush pink on the snows and ice of the east face, to think that this is where Monte Rosa got her name. But it is more likely that 'rosa' is instead derived from a local dialect meaning 'glacier'. The full scope of rock and ice, couloir, snow and serac is difficult to take in all at once; the mountain fills the horizon to overflowing, and deep groans and rumbles from the glaciers and rock remind you that however eternal it looks, the reality of the landscape can change.

That mutability is most obvious in the state of the glaciers that cling to the east face. While they are considerably diminished (the scale of the Belvedere moraines are testament to how the ice used to fill the valley), there is still a great deal of ice, and in 2001 glaciologists found a unique – and potentially dangerous – environment, with a glacial surge increasing the ice velocity and forming sub-glacial reservoirs and supraglacial lakes. Without careful management and monitoring of instability in the rock and steep glaciers on the east face itself, these could destabilise parts of the glacier, and threaten floods and damage to Macugnaga far below.

As with the other Italian valleys, geography and climate combine to limit the guarantee of a full view of the east face. With warm, damp air rising from the Mediterranean and the Po valley and pushing north, the altitude rises, and that warm air hits the 4500m wall of Monte Rosa and forms cloud. This has led to a damp but fertile climate in the Italian valleys (the greenery in contrast to the more arid Swiss valleys), but does mean that sometimes hikers are stuck looking at a panorama of cloud.

After half an hour, reach **Rif Skarteboden** (1515m, **30min**, refuge). After 45min from Macugnaga, the path flattens to a viewpoint, which takes in the magnificent east face of Monte Rosa. In another 15mins, the route joins a wide track. The waymarked path leaves and rejoins this track several times, so it is simpler to follow the track up to **Alpe Bill** (1700m, **1hr 5min**, cable car).

Alpe Bill to Rif Oberto Maroli — 2hr 55min, 5km, +1100m -5m

The path continues to ascend, tucked between Alpe Bill and the track. The track can be very disrupted and cut up from Alpe Bill, so it is wiser to take the footpath which shadows it, crossing and rejoining. At 25–30min beyond Alpe Bill, the path

Atmospheric conditions on the east face of Monte Rosa

up to Monte Moro leaves the track for good and cuts away left, signed for the TMR, Passo Monte Moro and Rif Oberto Maroli.

The path can feel steep and unrelenting, but is also blessed with incredible views of Monte Rosa as it traverses up the green hillside accompanied by waltzes of butterflies among the purple heather, alpenrose, and bilberry bushes.

At 2300m, 2hr 45min from Macugnaga, the path skirts below a winter chairlift station, then crosses and climbs parallel to a stream. At 2550m, go straight over a track and continue up, with the winter chairlift line to your right, and a winter ski-tow ahead and to the left. If there is significant snow cover or poor conditions, consider turning left and following the track up to the Rifugio.

In the upper reaches of the climb, particularly if there is poor visibility or snow, wayfinding can be difficult. Bear in mind that the route will keep the winter chair lift on the right for some of the way, and there may be visible orange posts. The path meanders its way along and up the rocks, often stepped with large slabs, until the **Rif Oberto Maroli** (2796m, **4hr**, refuge) appears up and to the left (the cable car station is **+5min** further on).

The **Rifugio** is named for two Italian climbers from the early 20th century: Paolo Maroli, a young mountaineer, and Gaspare Oberto, a famous mountain guide. The Anzasca valley and Monte Rosa's east face have long attracted mountaineers, with many CAI (Club Alpino Italiano) bivaccos and rifugios commemorating past members and fallen friends. The Capanna Marinelli and Marinelli couloir (the longest couloir in the Alps, on the east face) for instance, are both named for Damiano Marinelli, who died when climbing the couloir in 1881.

STAGE 7A

Monte Moro to Saas-Fee (low-level, official route)

Start	Rif Oberto Maroli (2796m)
Finish	Saas-Fee (1803m)
Walking time	5hr 20min
Distance	17.2km
Ascent	300m
Descent	1295m
High point	Passo Monte Moro (Madonna of the Snows) (2872m)
Variant	Stages 7 and 8, the high-level glacier route via Britanniahütte

This is the officially recognised route from Monte Moro to Saas-Fee, taking one day, instead of the high-level two-day option via the Britanniahütte (Stages 7 and 8). As it stays at a lower altitude, it is the best option for when the weather is poor, you are short on time, or if you want to avoid the glacier crossing.

Nevertheless, this is a walk with great variety and interest – not to mention far more facilities! Starting high, the route going over the Monte Moro pass and the first section of descent picks its way across and around enormous stone slabs. There are often pockets (or more) of snow to navigate. After this initial challenge, the walk drops down to run the length of Stausee Mattmark before dropping into forest paths that traverse gently down the valley towards Saas-Almagell. From this village, it's just a short uphill to Saas-Fee, and the striking cirque of the Mischabel peaks.

Rif Oberto Maroli to Passo Monte Moro (Madonna) **15min, 0.5km, +75m**

From the rifugio, head up the waymarked steps towards the cable car station (**5mins**). Before reaching the station building, bear right towards a small tarn and follow red and white paint marks and arrows up towards the pass. On a clear day, you will see the golden statue of the Madonna of the Snows high above with a silver ribbon of metal stairs leading up. Climb up to the Madonna, but rather than go straight over into Switzerland, retrace your steps a few metres and go east as the path continues with chains and some metal stairs to **Passo Monte Moro** (Monte Moro Pass) (2872m, **15mins**), which is a little further down and along the ridge. For information about Passo Monte Moro, see Stage 7.

Saas-Grund
1561m
Saas-Fee
1803m
Schwarzmies
3185m
Weissmies
4023m
Rottalhorn
3815m
Trifthorn
3396m
N
0
1
2
km
Bodmen
Saas-Almagell
Waldegg
1671m
Plattjen
Almagellerhorn
3327m
Rotblattgletscher
Mittaghorn
3143m
Plattenhorn
3324m
Cresta di Saas
Egginer
3367m
Sonnighorn
3488m
Furggbach
Saastal
Saaser Vispa
Felskinn
Augstkummenhorn
3419m
Britanniahütte
3027m
Eiju 1930m
Pizzo Scarone
3342m
Klein Allalin
3070m
Metro-Alpin (funicular-tunnel)
Chessjengletscher
Feegletscher
Mittelallalin
Hohlaubgletscher
Mattmark
2204m
Nollenhorn
3185m
Allalinhorn
4027m
Schwarzbergchopf
2869m
Stausee Mattmark
Nollengletscher
Allalingletscher
Jazzihorn
3227m
SWITZERLAND
Fluchthorn
3802m
Strahlhorn
4190m
Dischtlealp
2224m
Ofentalgletscher
Pizzo di Antigine
3189m
Talliboden
2484m
Schwarzberggletscher
Seewjinengletscher
Passo Monte Moro
2872m
Pizzo Mondelli
2958m
Tällibodengletscher
Rothhorn
3230m
Joderhorn
3036m
Schwarzberghorn
3610m
Seewjinenhorn
3206m
Rif Oberto Maroli
2796m
Rio Mondelli
Ghiacciaio di Roffel
ITALY
Faderhorn
2475m
Battel
2928m
Cima di Jazzi
3803m
Pecetto

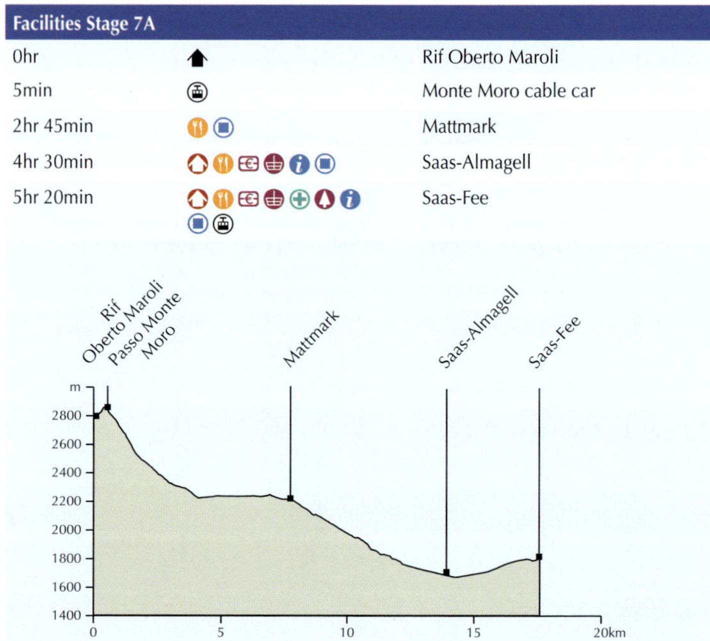

Facilities Stage 7A		
0hr		Rif Oberto Maroli
5min		Monte Moro cable car
2hr 45min		Mattmark
4hr 30min		Saas-Almagell
5hr 20min		Saas-Fee

Passo Monte Moro (Madonna) to Mattmark **2hr 30min, 7.2km, +45m -715m**

To descend from the pass, the route picks its way through tumbled boulders and across and between large, sloped rock slabs. In poor visibility or snow cover, the red-and-white waymarks will be very difficult to see so take care. After 350m of descent, just under an hour from the start, the path levels off, and you can take in the mountains before you, with the pyramid of the Bietschhorn in the far distance to the north, between the 'V' of the Saastal valley. Looking back, it is clear that you have descended down the steep slope of a U, carved out by a previous glacier over thousands of years.

An hour from the Madonna reach the river at **Talliboden** (2484m). Do not cross here, but continue left and down. In another half an hour, the descent path reaches the track which circumnavigates the **Stausee Mattmark** at Dischtlealp (2224m, **1hr 45min**). Here you have a choice. The left path will take you to Saas-Almagell and Saas-Fee (signed 2hr 50min and 3hr 50min respectively), and give you the option to join the high-level route across the glaciers to

Gentle walking in Saastal's forests

Britanniahütte. The path to the right will also take you through to Saas-Almagell and Saas-Fee, and is only about 15min longer.

The route left above the milky jade lake may be paved in tarmac, but it provides a welcome opportunity to stride out. The route around the lake is popular for all walkers, so expect to share the path with trail runners, mountain bikers and families. Continue alongside the shore of Stausee Mattmark and through (or above) a tunnel. At 35min from Dischtlealp, the high-level route (see Stage 7) splits off to the left (**2hr 20min**). To continue to **Mattmark**, pass through another tunnel, and reach the dam wall with a café-restaurant on the corner, and a bus stop adjoining (2204m, **2hr 45min**, refreshments, bus). From Mattmark, it is possible to get a bus to Saas-Almagell, and further to Saas-Fee.

MATTMARK

Since the construction of the dam in the 1960s, the lake at Mattmark has been a reservoir. However, before construction, there was a pre-existing lake formed by the Allalingletscher moraine blocking the Vispa river in a natural dam. But glacial landscapes are inherently unstable, and over the centuries the Saastal was subject to powerful floods as the waters of the lake broke through its moraine dam.

Stabilising the lake and tapping into its potential for generating hydro-electric power had been considered from the 1920s. By the 1950s, preparation began for construction of the current dam. The dam itself stretches across the upper Saastal valley for nearly 800 metres, and is constructed of moraine debris, making it the largest earth and rock dam in Europe. The reservoir now serves two purposes: generating power, and providing a control mechanism against floods that could devastate the Saastal. The Mattmark restaurant building has a small exhibition space about the dam.

In 1965, Mattmark was the site of one of the worst natural disasters in Switzerland: on 30th August, two million cubic metres of ice and rock broke from the Allalingletscher above the construction site of the dam. The avalanche swept through the cabins housing the constructions workers, and 88 people lost their lives.

Mattmark to Saas-Almagell **1hr 45min, 6.2km, +30m -565m**

The standard route crosses over the dam, where there are informational signs about the building and construction along the way. At the end of the dam, turn left signed to Saas-Almagell, 1hr 35min away.

If the descending path on the east side of the dam is closed (as it was in 2024), then follow the road from the Mattmark restaurant down the front of the dam. After 25min, and a large hairpin, take the footpath to the right, signed to Saas-Almagell. The onward path follows a wide grassy track through the trees, until a hairpin is reached whereupon you carry straight on, traversing the hillside. The footpath narrows, crossing streams and pastures before reaching the terraced farm buildings at **Eiju**, or Eienalp (1930m, no facilities).

The path turns left at the buildings, then right and continues into a forest. This is a very pleasant route as it traverses above the valley among trees and boulders, with the Saaser Vispa river roaring below. The path has regular pink signage, identifying it as a winter snowshoe route. After 35min from Eiju, the path drops down to the road. Saas-Almagell is signed right and the path shadows the road for the rest of the way. Take the road bridge across the Saaser Vispa, then immediately right on a grassy path which passes a small church, before soon rejoining the road. If you do not need to go to Saas-Almagell and the route is open, you can bear left on a track before crossing the second road bridge and continue on the left bank.

Cross the river again and follow the road, passing Pension Waldegg, the first refreshments and accommodation en route since Mattmark. In another 5min, reach the centre of **Saas-Almagell** (1671m, **4hr 30mins**).

Saas-Almagell

SAAS-ALMAGELL

Saas-Almagell is the most southerly of the Saastal villages, and remains the smallest and quietest. It retains many traditional buildings, and is tucked away in forest next to the Saaser Vispa, where the Leebach and Furggbach come tumbling down from the eastern chain of mountains that border Italy. It was relatively isolated throughout its history, but would have benefited from trade going over to Italy across the Passo Monte Moro.

The village has a range of accommodation options, as well as a small central square with grocery shop, bank, tourist information, and regular buses that run from Mattmark, through Saas-Almagell, to Saas-Grund and beyond.

Saas-Almagell to Saas-Fee

50min, 3.3km, +150m -15m

From the central square in Saas-Almagell, take the route left next to the food shop and cross the bridge. After the bridge turn right and take the path slanting up the hill (not the one that continues along the Saaser Vispa), signed to Saas-Fee. This broad and smooth track, a popular route for families and visitors to the Saastal, ascends gently up the hill. As the track eases around the curve of the hillside, you pass Restaurant Waldhüs Bodmen (1769m, refreshments).

Saas-Fee's traditional buildings

Continue onwards towards Saas-Fee with occasional views to the Saastal valley and Saas-Grund below. A few minutes further on and the view opens up ahead to the glaciers and peaks that surround Saas-Fee. When the track becomes a road, head right and down. At the next junction with the town of Saas-Fee directly ahead, turn right over the bridge and up into the town, and right again on reaching a collection of traditional alpine buildings, to the tourist information office and bus station in **Saas-Fee** (1803m, **5hr 20min**). For more details about Saas-Fee, see the information in Stage 8.

STAGE 7

Monte Moro to Britanniahütte (high-level glacier route)

Start	Rif Oberto Maroli (2796m)
Finish	Britanniahütte (3027m)
Walking time	6hr
Distance	14km
Ascent	1040m
Descent	810m
High point	Britanniahütte (3027m)
Variant	Stage 7A, the low-level, official route to Saas-Fee

Today's stage is a chance to venture high into the alpine world of snowy 4000-ers, glaciers, intricate paths and a true icon of an alpine refuge; not a landscape where many treks typically tread. If you are well prepared and the weather is clear, this is an immensely rewarding day with spectacular views up close to the giants of the Alps.

The route crosses two glaciers on the way to the Britanniahütte; that alone would recommend this route only to hikers who have experience with glaciers and the right equipment – no matter how 'user-friendly' these crossings are. To add to that, the climb up from Stausee Mattmark and the tricky route finding across glacial rubble is such that this route is only recommended in good, clear conditions – for the views if nothing else.

If conditions in the weather or for the glacier crossing are poor, it is recommended to take Stage 7A, the official lower-level route to Saas-Fee.

CROSSING GLACIERS

Glaciers are inherently unstable and should not be underestimated. Before choosing this route option, please see the 'Glacier crossing' section in the Introduction for advice and identifying safer conditions.

Rif Oberto Maroli to Passo Monte Moro (Madonna) **15min, 0.5km, +75m**

From the rifugio, head up the waymarked steps towards the cable car station (**5mins**). Before reaching the station building, bear right towards a small tarn and follow red and white paint marks and arrows up towards the pass. On a clear

Monte Rosa from the Monte Moro

Facilities Stage 7		
0hr		Rif Oberto Maroli
5min		Monte Moro cable car
6hr		Britanniahütte

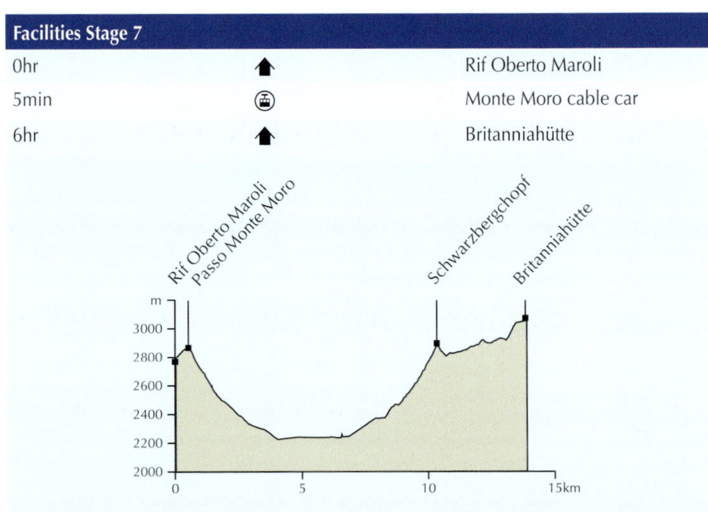

day, you will see the golden statue of the Madonna of the Snows high above with a silver ribbon of metal stairs leading up. Climb up to the Madonna, but rather than go straight over into Switzerland, retrace your steps a few metres and go east as the path continues with chains and some metal stairs to **Passo Monte Moro** (Monte Moro Pass) (2872m, **15mins**), which is found a little further down and along the ridge.

PASSO MONTE MORO

The Madonna of the Snows, gilded statue at the top of the Passo Monte Moro

Or 'Monte Moropass' in German, was, like the Theodulpass to the west, a historically crucial link between the Swiss Valais and Italy. The Walser migrations in the 13th century used the Monte Moro to travel south from the Saastal into the Anzasca valley (and thence to Alagna's Valsesia). However, unlike at Theodul, we know that some of this migration was instigated by the marriage of Godefroi, Count of Biandrate to Aldise, the daughter of a Valais lord who also owned land from her mother's side; by 1250 ownership of land on both sides of the Monte Moro meant that Godefroi and Aldise could resettle their serfs on either side of the mountain border.

In the Middle Ages, trade also prospered over the pass, and there are records of an established track allowing mule trains and horses to cross without issue, as well as providing for the transhumance movement of livestock from the Saastal to the sunnier Italian valley for winter. But by the middle of the millennium, the cooling climate of the Little Ice Age led to glaciers advancing and destroying the track; references from Monte Rosa tourers in the 1800s refer to the pass as a greater challenge than the Theodul, and that the route was no longer passable for horses and mules. But even so, trade (and smuggling), continued.

Now, the southern slopes of Passo Monte Moro are more dedicated to skiing, with the main cable car from Macugnaga joined by winter-only chairlifts and ski pulls. The northern side is comparatively wild, but the significance of the pass as a crucial crossing point is commemorated at the summit by the golden statue of the Madonna of the Snows (*Madonna delle Nevi*), who gazes down to Valle Anzasca and the east face of Monte Rosa. She is 4.6m high, cast in bronze, and is half-filled with concrete to hold her steady against the wind. Set up in 1966, the statue was later (in 1997) gilded in gold leaf to commemorate Macugnaga's gold mines. On the first Sunday of August every year, a mass is celebrated at Passo Monte Moro.

Saas-Almagell
1671m
Plattjen
Mittaghorn
3143m
Almagellerho
3327m
CRESTA D
Egginer
3367m
Furggbach
SAASTAL
Saaser Vispa
212.1
Augstk
Feegletscher
Felskinn
Chessjengletscher
Metro-Alpin (funicular tunnel)
Britanniahütte
3027m
Klein Allalin
3070m
Mittelallalin
Hohlaubgletscher
Mattmark
2204m
Nollenhorn
3185m
Allalinhorn
4027m
Schwarzbergchopf
2869m
Stausee Mattmark
Schwarzbergalp
2372m
Nolle
Melligletscher
Allalingletscher
SWITZERLAND
Rimpfischhorn
4199m
Fluchthorn
3802m
Dischtlealp
2224m
Ofentalgle
Pizzo di
Strahlhorn
4190m
Adlerhorn
3988m
Tälliboden
2484m
Schwarzberggletscher
Seewjinengletscher
Passo Monte Moro
2872m
Pizzo
Tälliboc
Rothhorn
3230m
Schwarzberghorn
3610m
Joderhorn
3036m
Seewjinenhorn
3206m
Rif Oberto Maro
2796m
Ghiacciaio di Roffel
Faderhorn
2475m
Batt
2928
Cima di Jazzi
3803m
Alpe Bill
1700m
Macugnaga
N
Pecetto
1315m
Staffa
VALLE
Torrente Anza
SP549
0
1
2
km

Passo Monte Moro to Schwarzbergchopf **3hr 50min, 10km, +655m -660m**

To descend from the pass, the route picks its way through tumbled boulders and across and between large, sloped rock slabs. In poor visibility or snow cover, the red-and-white waymarks will be very difficult to see so take care. After 350m of descent, just under an hour from the start, the path levels off, and you can take in the mountains before you, with the pyramid of the Bietschhorn in the far distance to the north, between the V of the Saastal valley. Looking back, it is clear that you have descended down the steep slope of a U, carved out by a previous glacier over thousands of years.

An hour from the Madonna reach the river at **Tälliboden** (2484m). Do not cross here, but continue left and down. In another half an hour, the descent path reaches the track which circumnavigates the **Stausee Mattmark** at Dischtlealp (2224m, **1hr 45min**).

Turn left on the route around the reservoir. The track above the milky jade waters may be paved in tarmac, but it provides a welcome opportunity to stride out. The route is popular, so expect to share the path with trail runners, mountain bikers and families. Continue alongside the shore of Stausee Mattmark and through (or above) a tunnel. After 35min from Dischtlealp, the high-level route leaves the lake track and splits off to the left, signed for the Britanniahütte in blue, 3hr 55min away (**2hr 20min**).

The route left doubles back uphill and rises on a steady gradient on a well-made track. Views open up ahead of the hillside that you descended from Monte Moro. After 20min from the turn, the track ends at **Schwarzbergalp** (2372m, **2hr 40min**) and the route onwards is signed left as it turns into a small and twisty path. The path climbs quickly and clambers up the steep nose of Schwartzbergchopf on a narrow path. For the final 250m of the climb, the path becomes slightly easier as it rises up the crest of the ridge in tight zigzags until the saddle of **Schwarzbergchopf** (2869m, **4hrs 5mins**). This high point on the Schwarzberggrat ridge has spectacular views, and you can see the route ahead across two glaciers and up to the far off Britanniahütte, perched high above the ice.

Schwarzbergchopf to Britanniahütte **1hr 55min, 3.5km, +310m -150m**

The route down to the **Allalingletscher** follows blue and white paint splashes down steep and tight zigzags, before leading onto glacier rubble. Before you know it, you'll be on the ice, and it's time to strap on spikes or crampons.

Take care across the glacier, it is not officially marked out, but the route that previous walkers have taken should be quite clear. There are crevasses on the glacier, so do not stray from the path. When you reach the substantial moraine separating the Allalingletscher from the Hohlaubgletscher, remove spikes and make

Crossing the Allalingletscher, with the path from the Schwarzbergchopf behind

your way over. At the top of the rubble, the blue-white waymarks can be thin on the ground, but you are aiming for roughly north-east where bare smooth rock is visible under the rubble. There will be visible blue and white markers on the next rise, which turn the route more north-north-west.

The blue and white markers occur every five to ten metres and the route picks its way across a field of boulders heading generally uphill. Eventually the boulders will end and you will cross smooth rock covered with rivers and gentle pools until you reach the edge of the **Hohlaubgletscher** and it is again time for spikes. The Hohlaubgletscher has a more obvious edge to the ice than the previous glacier but can be gained without great difficulty. There are also blue poles leading the way across.

After the second glacier is more boulder hopping, this time with fewer visible paint splashes. Finally, the grind of the path up to the hut that has been visible for some time is reached. The **Britanniahütte** (3027m, **6hrs**, refuge) at the top is a welcome finish with a panoramic sun terrace to take in the staggering views: the Fluchthorn, Stralhorn, Rimpfischhorn and Allalinhorn in particular dominating the scene.

To complete the route to Saas-Fee in one day, there is an option to continue past Britanniahütte to the Felskinn cable car station above Saas-Fee, adding 1hr to the time. Check the time for the last lift at www.saas-fee.ch, this is likely before 16.00

BRITANNIAHÜTTE

The Britanniahütte (3027m) stands three-stories tall and imposing on the small col along the Hinter Allalin ridge, next to the Klein Allalin (3070m, can be easily climbed in a few minutes from the hut). Owned by the Swiss Alpine Club, and originally funded by the Association of British Members of the Swiss Alpine Club, it is one of the most popular huts in Switzerland and also marks the start of the winter ski mountaineering Haute Route. Built in 1912, the hut has since been expanded and can now accommodate 101 people. In summer, the hut opens between mid June and mid September, and is most popular with mountaineers preparing to climb the Allalinhorn (4027m), other 4000-ers, or the nearby and popular Britannia via ferrata route.

Staying in a high alpine hut can be a unique experience. Many of the guests may have a very early start in the morning, so remember to be courteous and quiet. The Britannia has very limited water supplies, so expect that you will need to pay for all drinking water, and there are no showers. If you have time, experience, and want to get a new perspective on the surrounding mountains, via ferrata kit can be rented from the hut: the full excursion takes around 3hr from Britanniahütte.

Firey skies above the Dom from Britanniahütte

STAGE 8

Britanniahütte to Saas-Fee

Start	Britanniahütte (3027m)
Finish	Saas-Fee (1803m)
Walking time	3hr 40min
Distance	10.2km
Ascent	100m
Descent	1325m
High point	Britanniahütte (3027m)
Variant	1hr walk to Felskinn cable car to shorten

The descent down to Saas-Fee is a short stage, and could be made even shorter by taking the gondola lift from Plattjen or Felskinn to Saas-Fee. However, it is a stage that transitions from the high reaches of the Alps down to one of its favoured Swiss towns, through a rocky and boulder-tossed balcony route, down through meadows, and into cool and shaded woods. The path offers far-reaching views across the Saastal and through to the Rhône valley peaks, while Saas-Fee awaits surrounded by its enormous cirque of rock and ice.

For an even shorter day, or to compress Stages 7 and 8 into one day, there is a direct path to the Felskinn cable car station above Saas-Fee from Britanniahütte that can be reached in 1hr. Check www.saas-fee.ch for lift times, the last descent will be before 16.00.

Britanniahütte to Plattjen — 2hr, 4.7km, +75m -535m

The path begins on the eastern side of the sun terrace at the Britanniahütte, heading towards the Klein Allalin the path quickly splits off left from the saddle and skirts its way round and down across large glacier-polished slabs. After 25min, reach a signpost with Plattjen indicated off to the right: this is your onward route.

About half an hour from the hut, the path rises to the top of a crest of moraine and winds its way downhill before cutting left to join the main path towards Plattjen, which traverses the hillside. A few minutes further will be another signpost, keep left on the higher path towards Plattjen, rather than descend to Saas-Almagell.

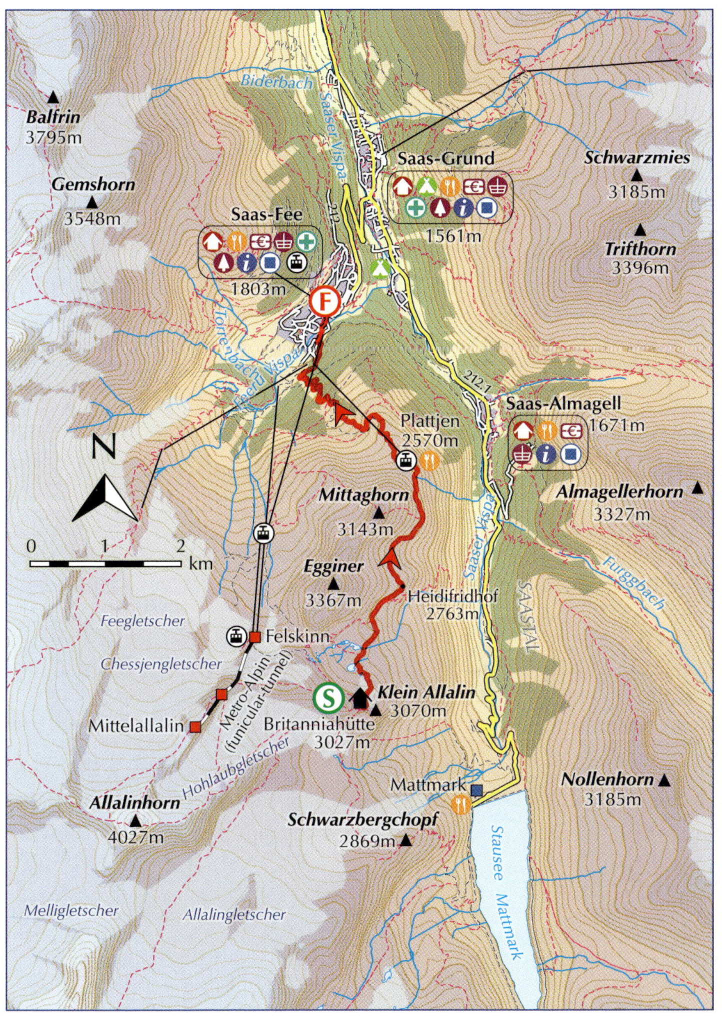
Biderbach
Saaser Vispa
Balfrin
3795m
Gemshorn
3548m
Saas-Grund
1561m
Schwarzmies
3185m
Trifthorn
3396m
Saas-Fee
1803m
212
Torrenbach
Feevispa
212.1
Saas-Almagell
1671m
Plattjen
2570m
N
Mittaghorn
3143m
Almagellerhorn
3327m
0
1
2
km
Egginer
3367m
Heidifridhof
2763m
Furggbach
SAASTAL
Feegletscher
Felskinn
Chessjengletscher
Metro-Alpin
(funicular-tunnel)
Klein Allalin
3070m
Mittelallalin
Britanniahütte
3027m
Hohlaubgletscher
Mattmark
Nollenhorn
3185m
Allalinhorn
4027m
Schwarzbergchopf
2869m
Stausee Mattmark
Melligletscher
Allalingletscher

Facilities Stage 8		
0hr		Britanniahütte
2hr		Plattjen
3hr 40min		Saas-Fee

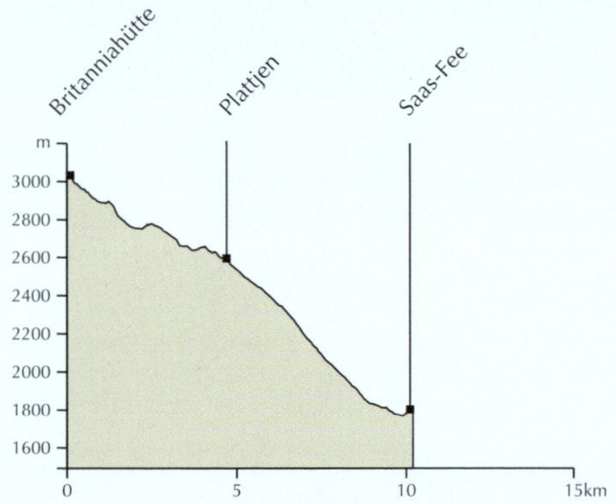

Britanniahütte
Plattjen
Saas-Fee
m
3000
2800
2600
2400
2200
2000
1800
1600
0
5
10
15km

Counter-intuitively, now the path has become a red–white hiking trail rather than blue–white alpine trail, it becomes a little more difficult. After a couple

Looking back to the Britanniahütte

of short, cabled sections, the path gently rises around the corner of the hillside towards the top of the rise near **Heidifridhof** (2763m). While you can go up to the high point, the path otherwise keeps to the left following red and white markers. The markers continue across a boulder field.

The path will smooth out and continue to traverse the hillside, generally down with occasional climbs. Roughly 1hr 40min into the walk you enter another large boulder field – keep an eye on all of the waymarks, you will be aiming for a stone cairn with the Swiss flag. From here it is just another five minutes to **Plattjen** (2570m, **2hrs**, refreshments, cable car).

Plattjen to Saas-Fee

1hr 40min, 5.5km, +25m -790m

The hillside beneath Plattjen is criss-crossed with paths that descend to Saas-Fee. The main route down continues to the left of the cable car station, descending in long zigzags at a good gradient. The gondola overhead is remarkably quiet and unobtrusive. In 20min, the Plattjen Berghaus restaurant (closed, no facilities) is passed and the route bears left. Half an hour from Plattjen there is a junction, with the direct route to Saas-Fee turning off to the right, which will shortly after enter into shaded forest. After 50min from Plattjen, you will reach a track with Saas-Fee Foreststrasse signed to the right. Instead, continue straight on, on the direct route.

After descending from Plattjen for 1hr 20min, you will reach a signpost at the edge of a meadow/piste, with Saas-Fee signed both straight on and to the left. It's recommended you go straight on, taking the Bodmenwasserleitung or Saas-Fee Gemsweg.

The path traverses high above Saastal, looking across valley to the Lagginhorn (left) and Weissmies (centre)

A little over 5min alongside the burbling water channel, a wooden sign will point you left to Saas-Fee. On reaching a track, turn right downhill. On the start of the tarmac, turn right and go downhill past the cable car station, before curving left over the bridge. The stage will end at the tourist office, so straight after the bridge turn right up a narrow footpath and onto a wider road leading to the centre of **Saas-Fee** (1803m, **3hr 40min**).

The **Bodmenwasserleitung** (broadly translated: water channel to Bodmen) is one of a series of paths in Saastal that accompany irrigation channels (leats, or *suonen* in the local parlance, *bisse* in French). The Valais is a particularly dry region, especially when compared to the verdant green of the Italian valleys the other side of the mountain chain; so residents have had to be inventive throughout history to ensure enough water could reach their pastures. Many of the channels you may see could date back to medieval times, but are as invaluable now as they were then.

Bear in mind that the next stage to Grächen has no facilities for the first 6hr, nor any accommodation en route, so it will be important to stock up in Saas-Fee for the next stage.

SAAS-FEEE

In the hanging valley above the Saastal, with the Feeru Vispa cutting a gorge through the centre, Saas-Fee sits cupped in the enormous cirque of the Mischabel range, with the Dom paramount in the mountain wall. It is a quintessentially Swiss-Alpine place, where mountaineers and summer skiers mingle alongside valley-based visitors: all here to enjoy the spectacular mountains in a charming town.

Like Zermatt, Saas-Fee is car-free, and is an excellent place to wander: amongst the larger chalet-style buildings, traditional centuries-old Walser barns still perch above vegetable gardens. There are plenty of restaurants, cafés and shops to while away some time, or, if you get the opportunity and your accommodation gives you a SaastalCard, taking the cable car up to Längflue or Felskinn gives an up-close view of the glaciers cloaking the Täschhorn and Dom.

As a well-established honey pot, there's a wide range of accommodation and refreshment options. Public transport to and from Saas-Fee is via the bus, which drops down the valley edge to Saas-Grund.

STAGE 9

Saas-Fee to Grächen

Start	Saas-Fee (1803m)
Finish	Grächen (1618m)
Walking time	7hr 10min
Distance	20.3km
Ascent	995m
Descent	1180m
High point	Stock (2362m)

This is a truly fabulous stage, surely one of the great balcony routes of the Alps. The views are sweeping and offer more and more opportunity to take in the full majesty of the Swiss Alps, as the Saastal mountains give way to those that tower above the Rhône valley, as well as further north to the Bernese Oberland, and our first view of the Mattertal giants again. As well as proving itself exceptional for its views, the path between Saas-Fee and Grächen is also extraordinarily pretty, pine forests and summer greens paving the way for the higher rocky stretches.

It is also fair to note that despite not being the longest, nor with the greatest ascent or descent, this is nevertheless one of the hardest days on the TMR, and much of that has to do with negotiating the frequently narrow path with the airy drop to the valley. This is not a route for anyone who is anxious about heights. However, if conditions are good and you venture on the Höhenweg, it is a truly rewarding day – a highlight of the Tour.

Saas-Fee to the Schweibbach footbridge **3hr 35min, 10.2km, +610m -310m**

From the tourist office, head up Parkstrasse towards the police station, following the town signs which indicate the Grächen Höhenweg. Follow these under a building, past the police station and continue to follow Swiss Route 6 / Grächen Höhenweg out of town. Today you will be following Swiss Routes 6 and 27 as they go from Saas-Fee, skirting round on the high balcony route to Grächen. On the road out of town, a sign indicates Grächen will be reached in 7hr 40min.

Swiss Route 27 is also called the Swiss Tour of Monte Rosa, and follows the TMR route from Saas-Fee to Grächen and on to Zermatt along the Europaweg. All the numbered Swiss Routes (look for the green numbered squares on

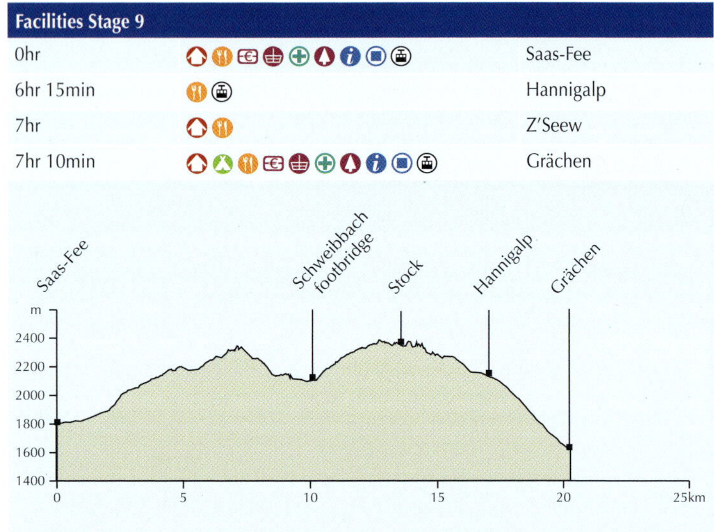

Facilities Stage 9	
0hr	Saas-Fee
6hr 15min	Hannigalp
7hr	Z'Seew
7hr 10min	Grächen

signposts) are routes wholly in Switzerland and do not go across borders, which is why only these three stages of the TMR are signed in this way. **Swiss Route 6** is known as the Alpine Passes Trail, a 695km-long epic from St Moritz to Lake Geneva.

The last buildings of Saas-Fee end at the edge of the forest (**15min**), with signs continuing to point the way. After another 15min, the track turns left at Bärufalla and a minute later the route is signed to the right up a small path into the forest. This is an exceptionally pretty climb, the forest cool and shaded as it rises, eventually the trees giving way to alpenrose and other fragrant shrubs. After 1hr 15min from the start, reach the **Balmeböden** junction where you will continue straight on Route 6. At the **Stafelalpji** junction (**1hr 40min**), this is the last opportunity to drop down to the valley and avoid the upcoming route. To continue, keep left, signed for Grächen in 5hr 50min.

The route now starts to present a few obstacles. After 2hr 20min from Saas-Fee there is a cable section with ladder before a large boulder field. Keep in mind the signs which warn of the danger of rockfall; unlike many of the previously covered boulder fields on this trek, this one definitely feels more unstable. Take care when crossing, following the yellow daubs or red/white paint splashes.

Stalden
Kalpetran
Hannigalp
2122m
Eisten
Mattwaldhorn
3246m
N
0
1
2
km
rächen
618m
Z'Seew
1721m
Wannehorn
2669m
Stock
2362m
Distelhorn
2830m
Gasenried
1660m
Seetalhorn
3036m
Rote Biel
2280m
Gabelhorn
3135m
Platthorn
3246m
Schweibbach
2102m
Saastal
Saaser Vispa
Riedbach
Lammenhorn
3190m
Schilthorn
3401m
Saas
Balen
Gross
Bigerhorn
3626m
Stafelalpji
2173m
Balfrin
3795m
Biderbach
Balmeböden
2123m
Riedgletscher
Bidergletscher
Saas-Grund
1561m
Gemshorn
3548m
Saas-Fee
1803m
Dirruhorn
4035m
Hohberghorn
4218m
Stecknadelhorn
4240m
Nadelhorn
4327m
Lenzspitze
4293m
Fee Vispa
Saas-Almagell
1671m
Dom
4546m
Mischabel
Plattjen
2570m
Mittaghorn
3143m
Täschhorn
4491m
Feegletscher

Hikers navigate a large boulderfield

Just after 3hr of walking, you will reach one of the headlands of the largest combe on the walk. The views across into the Rhône valley are as incredible to see as the long drop to the valley below. The combe dips westwards in a V towards the river, with the path winding through patches of sun and shade, pine trees and flowered shrubs lining the route. You cross the **Schweibbach** at the footbridge (2102m, **3hr 35min**), which also offers a good opportunity to refill water bottles.

THE MISCHABEL RANGE

The Mischabel range, or group, is the main ridgeline of peaks that forms the northern spur from Monte Rosa and divides the Saastal from the Mattertal. It includes eleven 4000m summits and is the highest massif of mountains wholly in Switzerland, with the mighty Dom paramount, best seen from Saas-Fee. These are the peaks which have dominated the past few days – particularly if your TMR led you to Britanniahütte – and will continue to cast morning shadows as you continue into the Mattertal. On Stage 9, it is the Balfrin that looms largest at the head of the bowls and hanging valleys along the route to Grächen.

Popular with climbers, the Mischabel range is peppered with bivouacs and mountain refuges (like the Britanniahütte) that have served and sheltered alpinists for over 100 years. Several of these are accessible for adventurous hikers.

Notable peaks of the range include:

- Dom (4545m)
- Täschhorn (4491)

- Lenspitze (4293m)
- Nadelhorn (4327m)
- Just outside the Mischabel range lies Balfrin (3795m, while there are several taller peaks, you'll be seeing this one a lot)

Schweibbach footbridge to Hannigalp **2hr 40min, 7km, +385m -365m**

From the bridge over the Schweibbach, the path traverses up the opposing hill, occasionally climbing quite steeply until you come to a bench on the crest of the headland – taking in the fantastic view behind you of the Balfrin, Lammenhorn, Schilthorn, and Gross-Bigerhorn.

From this headland point, named **Rote Biel** on the map, the path becomes truly spectacular as it traverses round the next mountain bowl. Be prepared for infrequent cabled protection, some very narrow sections, and warning of rock falls. This is the sort of walk that will demand all your focus: no matter how wonderful the view!

At the end of traversing this bowl, which will take about 1hr, you arrive at the **Stock** headland. From here, the next bowl has far more attached protection, and the path continues to have an airy outlook as it broadly descends.

The final section before Hannigalp is on blissfully flattish woodland leading to **Hannigalp chapel**, its glass walls looking out at the exceptional panorama; the Weisshorn to the left, with the Rhône valley and Oberland to the right. This is now the very top of the teardrop shaped Monte Rosa massif. From the chapel, it is a short walk down to the buildings at **Hannigalp** (2122m, **6hr 15min**) where you find some very welcome refreshments and the opportunity to take the cable car to Grächen.

Hannigalp chapel, or Hannigkapelle, was commissioned by the town of Grächen to replace the older, smaller chapel. Paul Anthamatten from Visp designed the modern church, and the construction work was largely undertaken by volunteers from Grächen in 1971. The chapel's patron saint is the Holy Brother Klaus, also known as Nicholas of Flüe, the patron saint of Switzerland. With the forest and Bernese Oberland as an altarpiece, the open design and use of local, natural materials creates a memorable and peaceful place.

Hannigalp to Grächen **55min, 3.1km, -505m**

To walk down, follow the signpost for Routes 6 and 27 down the track signed 1hr to Grächen. The track is wide and occasionally steep – keep an eye out for mountain

Trees cling to the cliffs and steep slopes above Saastal

bikers using the bike track on the right. Through much of the descent, there is a spectacular view of the Weisshorn and potentially the Matterhorn in the distance.

The highly picturesque lake of **Z'Seew** (1721m, **7hr**) is reached 45mins from Hannigalp, with a hotel/restaurant. If not staying here, continue on to **Grächen** down the track, dropping straight into the centre of town (1618m, **7hr 10min**), and enjoy a well-earned rest!

GRÄCHEN

Perched 500m above the valley floor on a sunny terrace, near the northern point of the mountain chain that juts like the bow of a ship between the Saastal and the Mattertal, sits the small Valaisian town of Grächen. Settled since neolithic times by hunters, for much of history, Grächen has been a small farming community, subject to various feudal lords and bishoprics. Grächen today attracts fewer visitors than Zermatt and Saas-Fee, and offers a warm welcome with far-reaching views up valley dominated by the Weisshorn. In early September, it hosts the start (and finish) of the UTMR trail races.

Grächen is a popular spot for hikers, mountain bikers and families in the summer, and has a good range of facilities including: accommodation options, grocery and outdoor shops, a pharmacy, bank, tourist information centre, and a local history museum. The town is partly car-free, and transport away from Grächen is by bus down to the train station in Sankt Niklaus in the valley.

STAGE 10

Grächen to Europahütte

Start	Grächen (1618m)
Finish	Europahütte (2264m)
Walking time	6hr 35min
Distance	17km
Ascent	1455m
Descent	805m
High point	path above the Birchbach (2340m)
Variant	If parts of the Europaweg are closed, drop down to walk along the footpaths in the Mattertal valley

You've reached the Mattertal again, the end at Zermatt is almost in sight, but you have two memorable days on the Europaweg ahead. Enjoy the easy first few kilometres south-west from Grächen: the rest of the walk will offer quite a challenge, but a spectacular one. Bridges, ramps, ladders, steps, ropes; all will be used as the path drops and climbs to reach the famed Europahütte. Expect stunning views of the Weisshorn and its neighbouring giants as the route weaves amongst forest, canyons and into the rocky reaches beyond the treeline. But be prepared for stern and steep paths, and a slightly busier route: you're now sharing the way with Chamonix–Zermatt Haute Route trekkers!

In bad weather, or if some or all of the Europaweg is closed, there is a route along the valley from St Niklaus, through Herbriggen, Randa and Täsch to Zermatt. This valley route up the Mattertal is 23km long, taking 5hr 30mins to Zermatt from St Niklaus and shadows the rail line for most of the way.

Grächen to Gasenried

35min, 2.4km, +65m -25m

In the central square at Grächen next to the church is a signpost, which indicates the Europahütte is 7hr away along Swiss Route 27 / the Europaweg. Follow this route south out of Grächen along the main road. After 15min, leave tarmac behind, and enter the trees on a wide forest track for a gentle and ambling start to the day.

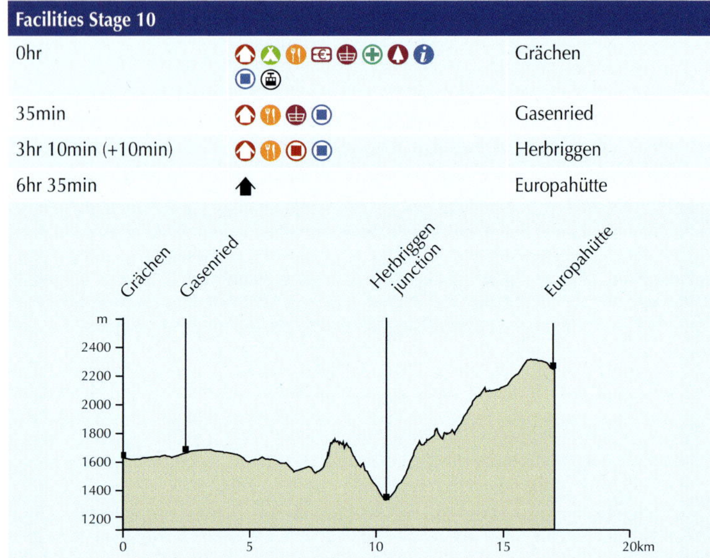

Facilities Stage 10	
0hr	Grächen
35min	Gasenried
3hr 10min (+10min)	Herbriggen
6hr 35min	Europahütte

The path will leave the trees and drop down to the road in the outskirts of **Gasenried** and continues up the hill towards the centre of the tiny and scattered village at a hotel and bus stop (1660m, **35min**).

THE EUROPAWEG

The Europaweg has been a labour of love since its opening in 2007, leading the full length of the eastern flank of the Mattertal in an effort to link Grächen, the Europahütte, Täschalp and Zermatt. Undeniably a stunning route, it has been beset by myriad difficulties of crumbling paths, rockfalls, and collapsing bridges. The terrain is notoriously fragile; the steep valley edge combining with eroded rock and the glaciers above, has led to rockfall prone boulder fields, tricky ravines, and mountain streams flowing full with meltwater. The wide assortment of cables, ladders, bridges, tunnels and ropes to aid trekkers is a testament to the ingenuity and investment of those who designed and maintain the route. Midway along the Europaweg, the Charles Kuonen Suspension Bridge – one of the longest suspension footbridges in the world – spans half a kilometre above a mountainside scarred by rockfalls.

The Europaweg can be subject to closures and route diversions: the whole initial section from Grächen to the Europahütte used to take a much higher route – but this was permanently closed several years ago due to the danger to walkers. It is important to check before you start the Europaweg for any closed sections as this may require dropping down to the valley.

It is hard to imagine, however, a better final two days to finish the TMR. The Europaweg makes the best of the Mattertal's views to the Weisshorn, Ober Gabelhorn and Zinalrothorn, with occasional glimpses above to the Mischabel peaks. The Matterhorn is often visible across the two days, gradually getting closer. Popular as a route on its own, and as part of Route 27 from Saas-Fee, the Europaweg is also the preferred path up the Mattertal for Chamonix Zermatt Haute Route hikers, the Tour of the Matterhorn, and, of course, the Tour of Monte Rosa.

Gasenried to junction above Herbriggen **2hr 35min, 7.7km, +315m -625m**

Leave Gasenried along the lane, and in another 10min, reach a track junction with Route 27 / the Europaweg and Europahütte signed 6hr 10min. From here, the lane descends down into the trees, becoming a track, and then a forest path.

After a period of downhill, 1hr 30min from Grächen, come to a signpost (1524m) where a path joins from the right, with Europahütte indicated straight on in 5hr 10min. After a further 20min, reach another junction at the edge of a ravine, the Grosse Grabe, with Route 27 and Europahütte signed left to the other side.

Shortly after the ravine, the path begins a merciless climb up through the trees, which will be aided in parts with steps and a useful rope you can use to haul yourself up. At about 1715m, turn off towards Herbriggen downhill. On the descent, you will pass behind the curtain of a spectacular waterfall of the Bielzigji stream.

The path will continue to descend steeply, passing occasional shrines, until you reach the **junction above Herbriggen** (1350m, **3hr 10min**). Here is an opportunity to drop down further into **Herbriggen** (1261m, **+10min off-route**, refreshments, accommodation, bus, train). However, the Europaweg beckons you onwards with a track to the left.

The junction above Herbriggen to Europahütte **3hr 25min, 6.9km, +1075m -155m**

Five minutes up from the Herbriggen junction, branch off the track towards a river/avalanche protection wall and follow this uphill. The path climbs through the forest in an uncompromising fashion, quickly gaining the height previously lost.

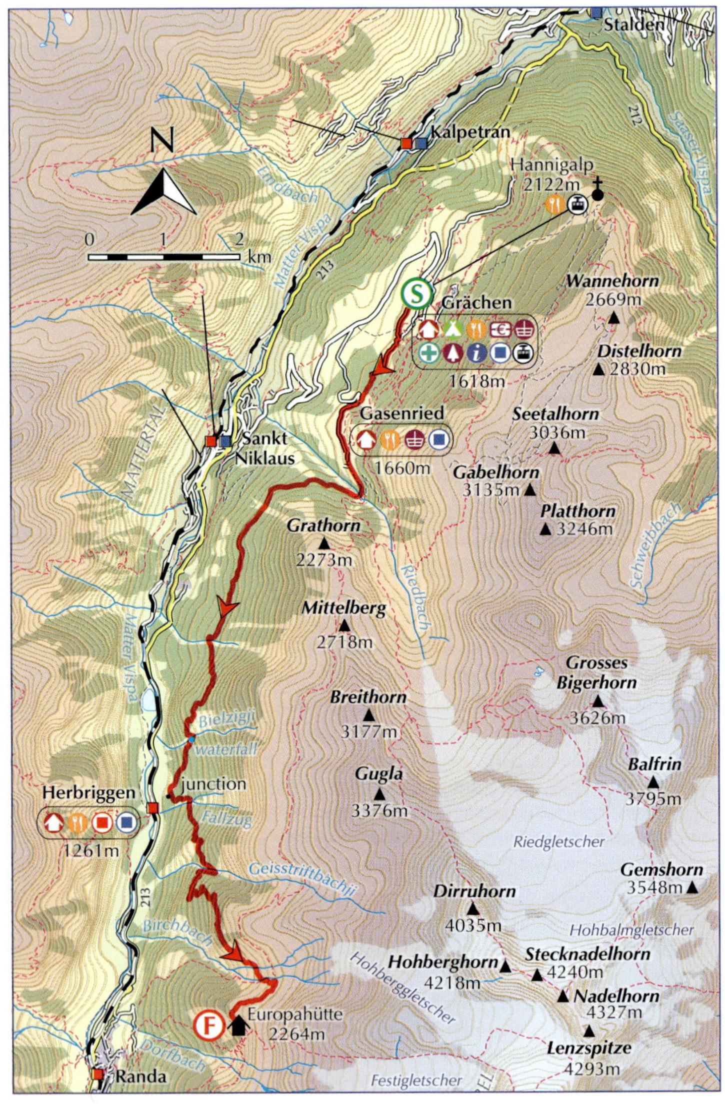
Stalden
Kalpetran
Hannigalp
2122m
Saaser Vispa
212
N
Emdbach
Matter Vispa
0
1
2
km
213
Grächen
1618m
Wannehorn
2669m
Distelhorn
2830m
Gasenried
1660m
Seetalhorn
3036m
Sankt
Niklaus
MATTERTAL
Gabelhorn
3135m
Platthorn
3246m
Grathorn
2273m
Schweibbach
Riedbach
Mittelberg
2718m
Matter Vispa
Grosses
Bigerhorn
3626m
Breithorn
3177m
Bielzigji
waterfall
junction
Herbriggen
1261m
Fallzug
Gugla
3376m
Balfrin
3795m
Riedgletscher
Gemshorn
3548m
Geisstriftbächji
Dirruhorn
4035m
213
Birchbach
Hohbalmgletscher
Hohberghorn
4218m
Stecknadelhorn
4240m
Hohberggletscher
Nadelhorn
4327m
Europahütte
2264m
Lenzspitze
4293m
Dorfbach
Randa
Festigletscher

The Europaweg passes a series of rock shrines on the descent to Herbriggen

Watch for red–white waymarks throughout, as minor paths split off from the avalanche protection. The path shortly requires a crossing (no bridge) of the Fallzug stream; this may be quite difficult if there's been heavy rain, so take care in finding a safe crossing place.

In 1hr 10min from the Herbriggen junction, you will hear the crash of a loud mountain river coming through the trees, and that will soon be joined by the sight of an enormous canyon wall in front of you, the **Geisstriftbächji** at its foot (1772m, **4hr 20min**). Turn uphill parallel to the river for a time, and then you'll see the way across: a bridge, followed by a sequence of steel stairs, which have been bolted to the cliff wall. Take note that only three people are allowed per section and keep a good distance between. Once up the stairs, the path follows the line of the canyon wall down for a time before bearing left and proceeding to climb steeply again, intricately picking its way up with sections of ramps, bridges, steps and rope for another 300m of ascent.

The path now contours around the hillside at around 2100m, this is an idyllic change of pace for a while, giving the opportunity to take in the view of the Weisshorn, especially as the path leaves the trees behind. The contour will end at the crossing of the main arm of the Birchbach over a bridge. Remember to fill up your water bottles if you can: the Europahütte, as a high alpine hut, will charge for water.

High above the river, you will see the faint outline of path which skirts the mountainside and heads over the next rocky crest. This is your path, and it will be one final climb to reach it. After the final 200m of ascent following the river crossing, you will reach the signpost with Europahütte signed just 25min away. Contour steadily across the mountain, the Weisshorn prominent in the view, taking care over loose rock. At the top of the crest is a spectacular viewpoint taking in the panorama. Carrying on, the path drops down, and soon Zermatt, then the famed suspension bridge, then finally the **Europahütte** come into view (2264m, **6hr 35min**, refuge). Be prepared for a busy arrival: you're now sharing the trail with the Chamonix to Zermatt route!

THE EUROPAHÜTTE

The Europahütte, operated by the Randa *gemeinde* (municipality), is a relatively new hut, built in 1999 amid larch forest at the limit of the treeline. The refuge has an unsurpassed view of the Weisshorn across the valley, where guests can expect a rosy glow as the morning light hits the snowy pyramid at breakfast time.

Open between mid June to mid or late September, the Europahütte is relatively small with 42 beds. It is nevertheless a very popular stop at the mid-section of the Europaweg. As such, you can expect your final night on

The Weisshorn gleams in the sun, with the remnants of the colossal rockfalls into the Mattertal

Dawn on the Weisshorn

the trail to be shared with Chamonix–Zermatt trekkers, and the rarer Tour of the Matterhorn or Europaweg trekker as well. The hut has a great, bustling atmosphere and is a memorable stay.

Keep an eye out for ibex grazing around the hut in the evening, and enjoy the long sweep of the view from the sun terrace. As the hut can get busy, early booking is advisable, showers are token-operated, and you may have overflow guests camping out on mattresses in the dining room.

STAGE 11

Europahütte to Zermatt

Start	Europahütte (2264m)
Finish	Zermatt (1616m)
Walking time	6hr 25min
Distance	19.5km
Ascent	765m
Decent	1420m
High point	2341m (before Tufteren)
Variant	If parts of the Europaweg are closed, drop down to walk along the Mattertal valley

The final day of the TMR is a spectacular day of walking, starting off with half a kilometre of suspension bridge under the bright arrowhead of the Weisshorn. The Europaweg continues to wind its way high above the Mattertal, with bridges, tunnels and protection cables lining the route, offering some challenge on this final stretch. The views will change hour by hour, as the walk cuts up a hanging valley to the high hamlet of Täschalp with the Rimpfischhorn at the head, and then finally to high above Zermatt, with views among the Zermatt 4000-ers again.

The descent down to the town stays quiet, among alpine pastures and forest tracks, before the final stretch to the bustling centre of town, and your pick of options to celebrate completing your Tour of Monte Rosa.

THE CHARLES KUONEN HÄNGEBRÜCKE

The Charles Kuonen Suspension Bridge is the longest pedestrian suspension bridge in the Alps, was the longest in the world at its opening, and is now the third longest in the world (as of 2025). It is 494m long and 85m above the ground at its highest point. Opening in 2017, the bridge cost 750,000CHF and is the latest of a progression of bridges spanning the Grabengufer: a rockfall-prone expanse of boulder fields coming down from the Festigletscher and Grabenhorn (3371m). It is a popular destination for walkers in the summer to hike up from Randa and see the graceful silver curve of the bridge above tumultuous terrain. The bridge should be avoided in thunderstorms.

Herbriggen
Fallzug
Bruneggh orn
3831m
Geisstriftbach
Dirruhorn
4035m
Birchbach
Matter-Vispa
Hohberggletscher
Bisgletscher
Europahütte
2264m
Domhütte
2937m
Hohgwächte
3739m
N
Randa
Dorfbach
Charles Kuonen Hängebrücke
Festigletscher
0
1
2
km
Specktbaum
2224m
Kinhütte
2581m
Grabenhorn
3371m
Wildibach
Troäre
2396m
Schalibach
Leiterspitzen
3409m
Täschbach
Täsch
Rotbach
Täschalp
2175m
Mettelhorn
3410m
Täschhütte
2701m
Sattelspitz
3162m
Bösentrift
3253m
MATTERTAL
Matter Vispa
Mellichbach
Tufteren
2215m
Ober
Rothhorn
3418m
Fluehorn
3317m
Triftbach
Zermatt
1616m
Unterrothorn
3103m
Funicular
(tunnel)
Sunnegga
2288m
Pfulwe
3314m
Zmuttbach
Gornergrat railway
Findelbach
Furi
1862m

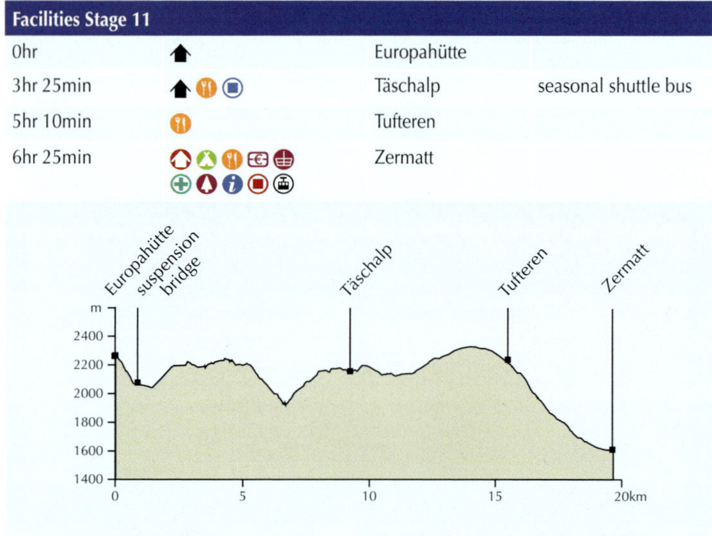

Facilities Stage 11			
0hr		Europahütte	
3hr 25min		Täschalp	seasonal shuttle bus
5hr 10min		Tufteren	
6hr 25min		Zermatt	

Europahütte to Täschalp

3hr 25min, 9.2km, +505m -600m

Leaving the Europahütte, the trail descends roughly 180m down to the start of the suspension bridge (**Charles Kuonen Hängebrücke**, 2080m, **20min**). This incredible feat of engineering allows quick passage across an enormous and rockfall-prone scree slope. Take care when crossing, it's a long way and the bridge has some movement to it; if you don't like heights, just try and look directly in front of you. Both before and after the bridge, there are options to drop down to the valley at Randa.

After the bridge, the path contours round and in a few minutes the Europaweg and Zermatt are signed to the left uphill. Further signs continue to point uphill, and after regaining the height lost to cross the bridge, the path will contour around the mountain side with wonderful views of the Zinalrothorn and the tip of the Matterhorn.

The contouring ends with a steep, roped section, which will then lead to the **Specktbaum junction** (2224m) where the route bears right. The way leads down some wooden steps and curves into a deep mountain bowl, the rocks rusted red. The path soon passes through a tunnel – it may be useful to have your headtorch or phone to hand but the tunnel isn't long – then continues to skirt the bowl with roped sections and wooden ramps helping the way.

The Charles Kuonen Suspension Bridge

Following the traverse of the bowl, the path continues to snake round the mountainside, with a variety of rockfall warnings and defences built in, before descending in several zigzags and eventually reaching a series of three tunnels underneath rumbled boulders. In 2024, the third tunnel was partially crushed and had a very low entrance; your rucksack will need to be carried, but it does get better. Alternatively, you may need to scramble over the scree. Ask the staff at Europahütte about the conditions of this section of the route before you go.

The five minute climb after the tunnels reaches a junction where there is an opportunity to drop down to Täsch if you need to. Otherwise, the Europaweg and Zermatt are signed onwards and up the hill, 4hr away.

The path continues to contour high above the Mattertal, gaining height. A number of zigzags take the path up and round the curve of the deeper V towards Täschalp. As the path levels you have the Rimpfischhorn ahead, the Matterhorn to the right, and the Weisshorn behind. Continue on through the lovely high pastures towards Täschalp. A stream crossing along the route may have a small diversion to gain a better crossing point, but the path reconnects shortly after. On reaching the small road, turn left into the centre of the hamlet of **Täschalp** (2175m, **3hr 25min**, refreshments, accommodation, occasional bus).

Täschalp is a pretty alpine hamlet, high in the Täschalpa hanging valley formed by the Rotbach and Mellichbach streams as they tumble down from the glaciers of the Mischabel group. There are options for a peaceful lunch

Approaching Täschalp with the Rimpfischhorn above

or an overnight stay at the Täschalp Restaurant and Lodge. Further off, and requiring 3km and over 500m of ascent to get there, is the stunningly positioned Täschhütte. There is also a minibus/taxi that serves Täschalp three times a day if you need to drop down to the valley.

THE MATTERTAL'S WESTERN PEAKS

Throughout the two-day walk along the Europaweg, the views are dominated by the western wall of the Mattertal valley. Despite looking impenetrable with 800m tall cliffs and the rubble of immense rockfalls, there are a number of paths that cling to the sides of the western slopes, but, like the Europaweg, they are prone to closure and crumbling terrain, and are less frequently travelled.

Forming a saw-toothed horizon above the forests and rock is a long chain of mountains that trails from the Italian border down to the Rhône valley, and stands between 2000–3000m above the floor of the Mattertal. The Weisshorn, at 4505m, is the grandest of the western peaks, and is well named for the snowy gleam of its north-eastern face that gives it an evocative beauty throughout the year. Between the Weisshorn and Randa in the valley is the scar of an enormous series of rockfalls that occurred in 1991. Around 30 million cubic metres of rock destroyed farms and homes, temporarily dammed the Matter Vispa, and required road and rail lines to be rerouted from where they had been buried. Luckily, no one was killed during these rockslides, and the area is under continuous monitoring for further danger.

Further south and up-valley from the Weisshorn are the more angular 4000m peaks of the Zinalrothorn (4221m) and the Ober Gabelhorn (4063m) that stand west of Zermatt itself. All three of these peaks were first climbed during the Golden Age of Alpinism in the 1860s, and remain very popular with mountaineers today. The chain eventually reaches the Italian border at the Tête Blanche, south of the Dent Blanche and west of the Matterhorn, and forms part of the cirque around the Zmutt valley.

Täschalp to Zermatt — 3hr, 10.3km, +260m -820m

The Europaweg leaves Täschalp off to the right by going down to cross the Mellichbach and zigzagging up to join the level path that you will see skirting around the hillside. This section leading out of Täschalp is some of the most pleasant and easy walking of the day. After half an hour, a junction gives you the opportunity to descend to Täsch, otherwise continue straight on and in another 10min reach a junction with a track on a hairpin. While Zermatt appears quite close at this point, rather than descend, take the left uphill track.

The track gains height quite quickly and then turns into a path which continues to gently climb until a stunning viewpoint is reached at 2335m with panoramic views from all sides. From here it's 20mins down the track to **Tufteren** (or Tuftra) and its well-situated bar (2215m, **5hr 10min**, refreshments). Zermatt is now only 1hr 15min away, and 600m below.

From Tufteren, the path descends into shaded woods before going steeply down alongside a ski piste. Keep an eye out at the bottom for speedy mountain bikers where you will cross over a mountain biking track. Continue down through

The Castor, Pollux and Breithorn above Gornergrat

the forest, meeting a track where Route 27 indicates left downhill. A minute later the walker's path diverts from the track (used by mountain bikers) slightly left, running in parallel to the wider track.

Just above the first houses fringing Zermatt, reach a wider path with Route 27 to the right (although Zermatt's church and our finishing point is also signed

left). Turn right and descend in another few zigzags until you reach a tarmac road where you can turn left: signs are few and far between once you enter the town, but following the same road down to the river, crossing, and climbing the other side will reach **Zermatt's** central square by the church, and the end to your Tour of Monte Rosa (1616m, **6hr 25min**).

APPENDIX A

Accommodation

This list details accommodation in sequential order when following the TMR as described in this guide, starting with Zermatt. The number of places, type of accommodation on offer, and seasonal open dates are given when known. Further information is available from local tourist offices (see Appendix B). Updates, additions and alterations are welcomed by the author.

Note: international dialling codes for Switzerland are (+0041) and for Italy are (+0039).

Stage	Name	Type	Facilities	Open
Switzerland				
1	Zermatt Youth Hostel		170 beds in 47 rooms, including private rooms	
1	Hotel Carina, Zermatt		Hotel rooms, plus 12 dormitory beds	
1	Hotel Bahnhof, Zermatt		Private rooms and dormitory beds	
1	Hotel Rhodania, Zermatt			
1	Camping Zermatt			Early June to end September
1	Silvana Mountain Hotel, Furi			
1	Gandegghütte		50 beds in 7 dormitories	End June to mid September
Italy				
2	Rifugio del Teodulo (Theodulhütte)		60 beds in 9 rooms and dormitories	Early to mid June to m September
2	Appartamenti Bettaforca, Saint-Jacques			June to September
2	Rifugio Ferraro, Resy		24 beds in 5 rooms	1 June to end Septemb
2	Rifugio Guide di Frachey, Resy		28 beds in 2 dormitories; 12 beds in 2–4 person private rooms	June to September
3	Hotel Ristoro Sitten, Sant'Anna		15 beds in 7 rooms	1 July to mid Septemb

hotel refuge/hut unmanned hut camping

Tel	Web/email	Comments
027 967 2320	www.youthhostel.ch / zermatt@youthhostel.ch	
027 966 4066	https://carinazermatt.ch	
027 967 2406	hotelbahnhofzermatt.com / welcome@hotelbahnhofzermatt.com	Meals not included
027 966 3410	www.rhodania-zermatt.ch / info@rhodania-zermatt.ch	
079 536 4630	www.campingzermatt.ch / info@campingzermatt.ch	Tent rental available
027 966 2800	http://hotelsilvana.ch / info@hotelsilvana.ch	
079 607 8868	www.gandegg.ch / info@gandegg.ch	No showers; bottled water must be bought
016 694 9400	www.rifugioteodulo.com / info@rifugioteodulo.com	No showers; bottled water must be bought
012 530 8764	https://bettaforca.com / info@betttaforca.com	Off-route in Saint-Jacques
328 328 5050	www.rifugioferraro.it / info@rifugioferraro.it	
334 746 3640	www.frachey-services-champouloc.it / infofrachey@gmail.com	
0125 366 300	www.sitten.it / info@sitten.it	

Stage	Name	Type	Facilities	Open
3	Ellex Eco Hotel, Stafal			
3	Hotel Nordend, Stafal			
3	Albergo del Ponte, Alpe Gabiet		25 beds in 10 rooms	Summer
3	Rifugio Gabiet, Alpe Gabiet		14 rooms with 2 to 4 beds	Summer and Winter
3	Oresteshütte		25 beds in 8 rooms	End June to mid September
4	Rifugio Zar Senni, Follu		14 beds in 5 rooms	June to mid September
4	Indren Hus Hotel, Alagna			
4	Hotel Cristallo, Alagna			
4	Campeggio Alagna Alagna		Tent pitches, cabins	
4	Rifugio Pastore		55 beds in rooms and dormitories	June to September
5	Bivacco Lanti		9 beds (+3)	
5	Hotel Dufour, Macugnaga			
5	Dream Hotel, Macugnaga			
5	Macugnaga Natural Camping			
6	Rifugio Scarteboden		21 beds in 5 rooms	
6	Rifugio Oberto Maroli, Monte Moro		24 beds in 5 rooms	Late June to late September
Switzerland				
7	Britanniahütte		101 dormitory beds	Late June to mid September
7A	Pension Restaurant Waldegg, Saas-Almagell			

Tel	Web/email	Comments
0125 366 637	www.ellexhotel.it / info@ellexhotel.it	
0125 366 807	www.hotelnordend.com / info@hotelnordend.com	
125 189 7137 / 347 697 9623	www.albergodelponte.com / info@albergodelponte.com	
125 189 1506 / 333 980 3655	www.rifugiogabiet.it / info@rifugiogabiet.it	
125 192 5484	www.oresteshuette.eu / info@oresteshuette.eu	Vegan, 50min off-route
0163 922 952	www.facebook.com/RifugioZarSenni / zarsenni.rifugio@gmail.com	
0163 91152	www.indrenhus.it / info@indrenhus.it	
0163 326 460	www.cristalloalagna.com / info@cristalloalagna.com	
0163 922 947	www.campeggioalagna.it / info@campeggioalagna.it	Minimum 2 nights for cabins
0163 326570	www.rifugimonterosa.it / info@rifugimonterosa.it	10 spaces for tents available; online booking
	https://caimacugnaga.org	Unmanned bivouac, very limited facilities; gas stove may be available
392 368 6271	www.hoteldufour.com / info@hoteldufour.com	
349 785 5758	www.dreamhotelalp.it / dreamhotelalp@gmail.com	
0324 740 003	https://naturalcamping.ossola collection.com / prenotazioni@ossolacollction.com	Tent rental available
939 338 769 / 939 016 936	www.facebook.com/scarteboden. rifugio	30min beyond Macugnaga
0324 65544	www.montemoropass.it / valcot.rifugio@gmail.com	Additional charge for showers
27 957 2288	www.britannia.ch / info@britannia.ch	No showers; bottled water must be bought
77 486 2665	https://pensionwaldegg.com / pensionwaldegg@hotmail.com	10min south of Saas-Almagell

Stage	Name	Type	Facilities	Open
7A	Hotel Monte-Moro, Saas-Almagell			
7A / 8	Kapellenweg Camping, Saas-Grund			Mid May to mid Octob
7A / 8	Wellness Hostel 4000, Saas-Fee		168 beds in 51 rooms, including private rooms	
7A / 8	Guesthouse Berggeist, Saas-Fee			
7A / 8	Hotel Christiania, Saas-Fee			
9	Hotel Zum See, Z'Seew			
9	Rooms Chez BeNi, Grächen			
9	Mountain Lodge, Grächen			
9	Camping Grächbiel, Grächen		Tent pitches, single and double rooms	Summer and winter
10	B&B Alpenrösli, Gasenried			
10	Hotel Bergfreund, Herbriggen			
10	Europahütte		42 dormitory beds (+overflow mattresses)	Mid June to mid September
11	Täschalp Restaurant and Lodge			Mid June to end September
11	Täschhütte		73 beds in 8 rooms	Mid June to late September
11	Zermatt (see start of list)			

Tel	Web/email	Comments
027 957 1012	www.monte-moro.ch / info@monte-moro.ch	
027 957 4997	www.kapellenweg.ch / camping@kapellenweg.ch	Off-route. 40min from Saas-Almagell; 30min from Saas-Fee (45min on return)
027 958 5050	www.youthhostel.ch / wellnesshostel4000@youthhostel.ch	
027 530 5015	https://berggeist-saas-fee.ch / info@lesamis-saas-fee.ch	No breakfast, online check-in, keys at Hotel Les Amis
027 957 3166	https://hotelchristiania.ch / info@hotelchristiania.ch	SaastalCard included in price
027 956 2424	www.hotel-zum-see.ch / info@hotel-zum-see.ch	10min above Grächen
077 403 8181	https://chez-beni.ch	
079 342 5119	https://www.mountain-lodge-grächen.ch	
078 622 1517	https://www.camping-graechbiel.ch / info@camping-graechbiel.ch	
078 217 7259	https://www.bnb-alpenroesli.ch / info@bnbalpenroesli.ch	
027 955 2323	https://hotel-bergfreund.ch / info@hotel-bergfreund.ch	10min off-route
027 967 8247 / 079 291 3322	www.randa.ch / europahuette@sunrise.ch	Additional charge for showers
027 967 2301	https://taeschalp.ch / info@taeschalp.ch	
027 967 3913	https://taeschhuette.ch / info@taeschhuette.ch	1hr 30min off-route with 500m ascent

APPENDIX B

Useful contacts

Weather and trail conditions

www.meteoswiss.admin.ch

www.mountain-forecast.com

https://map.schweizmobil.ch

Tourist information

Zermatt
Bahnhofplatz 5, 3920 Zermatt
+41 27 966 81 00
info@zermatt.swiss
www.zermatt.ch/en

Gressoney-la-Trinité
Località Tache, 11020 Gressoney-la-Trinité
+39 (0)125 366143
gressoney@turismo.vda.it
www.gressoneymonterosa.it/en

Alagna
1 Piazza Grober, 13021 Alagna Valsesia
+39 (0)163 922 988
ask@alagna.it
www.alagna.it/en

Macugnaga
Piazza Municipio 6, 28876 Macugnaga
+39 (0)324 65119
iat@comune.macugnaga.vb.it
https://macugnaga-monterosa.com

Saas-Almagell
Dorfplatz, CH-3905 Saas-Almagell
+41 27 958 18 88
info@saas-almagell.ch
www.saas-fee.ch/en

Saas-Fee
Obere Dorfstrasse 2, CH-3906 Saas-Fee
+41 27 958 18 58
info@saas-fee.ch
www.saas-fee.ch/en

Grächen
Dorfplatz, CH-3925 Grächen
+41 27 955 60 60
info@graechen.ch
https://graechen.ch/en

Alpine and Mountaineering Clubs

Club Alpino Italiano (CAI)
www.cai.it

Club Alpin Suisse (CAS)
www.sac-cas.ch/en

British Mountaineering Council (BMC)
www.thebmc.co.uk

Mountain guides (glacier crossing or other expeditions)

Zermatters
Bahnhofstrasse 58, CH-3920 Zermatt
+41 27 966 24 66
info@zermatters.ch
www.zermatters.ch/en

Maps

Stanfords
7 Mercer Walk, Covent Garden, London, WC2H 9FA
www.stanfords.co.uk

Cordee
www.cordee.co.uk

The Map Shop
15 High Street, Upton-upon-Severn, WR8 0HJ
www.themapshop.co.uk

ITMB
12300 Bridgeport Road, Richmond, BC, Canada
+1 604 273–1400
https://itmb.ca

Travel

Flights
Swiss International Airways
www.swiss.com

Easyjet
www.easyjet.com

British Airways
www.britishairways.com

Trains
EuroStar
www.eurostar.com

Swiss rail (SBB)
www.sbb.ch/en

TrenItalia
www.trenitalia.com/en

Trainline (multi-country booking)
www.thetrainline.com

Buses
Swiss PostBus
www.postauto.ch/en
www.sbb.ch/en

Taxi/bus to Täschalp, Mattertal
https://www.zermatt.ch/en/Media/Attractions/Taeschalp

Local buses Valle d'Ayas and Gressoney
www.vitagroup.it

Local buses Alagna Valsesia
www.baranzelli.it
www.alagna.it/en/shuttle-service

Local buses Macugnaga, Valle Anzasca
www.comazzibus.com

Airport minibus transfers
Arriva (Milan to Valle d'Aosta)
https://aosta.arriva.it/en

Comazzi Alibus (Milan to Domodossola)
www.comazzialibus.com

Specialist insurance providers
AAC members only:
Austrian Alpine Club
01929 556 870
https://www.alpenverein.at/britannia
(membership carries automatic accident and rescue insurance)

BMC members only:
BMC Travel and Activity Insurance
0161 445 6111
www.thebmc.co.uk

Harrison Beaumont Ltd
0345 450 8547
www.hbinsurance.co.uk

Snowcard Insurance Services
assistance@snowcard.co.uk
www.snowcard.co.uk

Dogtag Travel Insurance
0333 005 1085
www.dogtag.co.uk

APPENDIX C

Further reading

Mountaineering

Alps 4000: 75 Peaks in 52 Days by Martin Moran (David & Charles, Devon 1994) – The fascinating account of Moran's and Simon Jenkins's epic journey across all the 4000m summits of the Alps in one summer.

Scrambles Amongst the Alps by Edward Whymper (first edition 1871, numerous editions since, it's almost always in print) – Best-known for the story of the tragic first ascent of the Matterhorn, this book also recounts Whymper's other climbs. A much-respected volume, recommended to all would-be mountaineers.

The High Mountains of the Alps by Helmut Dumler and Willi P Burkhardt (Diadem, London 1994) – Sumptuously illustrated in colour throughout, this large-format volume is more than a 'coffee-table book', for it has an intelligent text which describes all the Alpine 4000m peaks, including those of the Monte Rosa range.

Narrative and travelogue

The Mountain Hut Book by Kev Reynolds (Cicerone, Kendal 2018) – An entertaining and informative book that looks at mountain huts and the hutting experience across the Alpine range. Lavishly illustrated throughout.

A Lady's Tour Round Monte Rosa by Mrs Henry Warwick Cole (Longman Brown Green Longmans and Roberts, 1859) – Currently available as an eBook. A fascinating insight into early tours around Monte Rosa taking place between 1850 and 1858; trekking during the high point of the Golden Age of Alpinism.

Summer Months Among the Alps: With the ascent of Monte Rosa by Thomas Woodbine Hinchliff (Longman Brown Green Longmans and Roberts, 1857) – Currently available as an eBook. Thomas Hinchliff was President of the Alpine Club between 1875–77, this book documents his earlier travels to the Monte Rosa region.

Other outdoor guides

Trekking in the Alps edited by Kev Reynolds (Cicerone Press, Milnthorpe 2019) – A sumptuously illustrated celebration of 20 of the finest multi-day tours in the Alps, including the TMR.

Walking in Zermatt and Saas-Fee by Jonathan and Lesley Williams (Cicerone Press, Kendal 2019) – Contains 50 day walks in the Mattertal and Saastal.

Walking in the Aosta Valley by Andy Hodges (Cicerone Press, Kendal 2022) – Contains 32 days walks in and around the Aosta valley.

Trekking the Giants' Trail: Alta Via 1 through the Italian Pennine Alps by Andy Hodges (Cicerone Press, Kendal 2021) – 180km trail from Donnas to Cormayeur above Aosta.

Italy's Grande Traversata delle Alpi by David Jordan (Cicerone Press, Kendal 2023) – 809km epic trail from Italy's Swiss border to the Mediterranean.

APPENDIX D

Italian–German–English glossary

Italian	German	English
acqua potabile	*Trinkwasser*	drinkable water
acqua non potabile	*Kein Trinkwasser*	non-drinkable water
aiuto!	*Hilfe!*	help!
aperto / chiuso	*Geöffnet / geschlossen*	open / closed
bivacco	*Biwak*	unmanned hut
cabinovia, telecabina	*Umlaufbahn*	gondola lift
capella	*Kapelle*	chapel
capitello	*Wegkreuz*	shrine
carta	*Karte*	map
cascata	*Wasserfall*	waterfall
cengia	*Band*	ledge
cima	*Gipfel*	mountain peak
croce	*Kreuz*	cross
destra / sinistra	*rechts / links*	right / left
diga	*Staumauer*	dam
dormitorio	*Schlaffsal*	dormitory
fermata	*Haltestelle*	bus stop
fiume	*Fluss*	river
forcella, passo, colle	*Scharte*	mountain pass
funicolare	*Standseilbahn*	funicular railway
funivia	*Seilbahn*	cable car
galleria	*Tunnel*	tunnel
ghiacciaio	*Gletscher*	glacier

Italian	German	English
giro	*Rundgang*	circuit
lago	*See*	lake
locanda	*Gasthof*	guesthouse
mezza pensione	*Halbpension*	half-board
navetta	*Pendelverkehr*	shuttle bus
nevaio	*Firnfeld*	snow field
orario	*Fahrplan*	timetable or opening hours
panificio	*Bäckerei*	bakery
pericolo	*Gefahr*	danger
ponte	*Brücke*	bridge
previsioni del tempo	*Wettervorhersage*	weather forecast
punta, pizzo, corno	*Spitze, Horn*	peak
rifugio	*Hütte*	manned mountain hut with food / accommodation
rio, torrente	*Bach, Wildbach*	stream, mountain stream
scorciatoia	*Abkürzung*	short cut
seggiovia	*Sessellift*	chairlift
sentiero	*Weg, Steig*	path
sentiero attrezzato	*Gesicherter Wandersteig*	aided path
sopra	*ober*	upper/above
sotto	*unter*	lower/below
stazione	*Bahnhof*	railway station
val, valle	*Tal*	valley

NOTES